The Energy Education Experts

Thank you for your purchase of *Understanding Today's Natural Gas Business*. If you wish to purchase additional copies of this book, please visit our website at www.enerdynamics.com. Or call us at 415.777.1007. Volume discounts start at as few as 25 books.

Please look for the newest addition to our line of books: *Understanding Today's LNG Business*, which is expected in November of 2005. Please also look for this book's electric companion, *Understanding Today's Electricity Business*. As with our gas book, this presents a comprehensive overview of the electricity industry in simple and easy-to-understand language. Priced at $69.95, it is the perfect primer for those new and not-so-new to the industry, and a valuable reference for years to come.

We also invite you to experience other learning opportunities available from Enerdynamics. These include public and in-house seminars, self-paced online training and our free *Energy Insider* newsletter. Learn more about all these products at www.enerdynamics.com.

Understanding Today's
Natural Gas Business

By Bob Shively and John Ferrare

The Energy Education Experts

P.O. Box 411165
San Francisco, CA 94141-1165
415.777.1007
www.enerdynamics.com

Enerdynamics LLC

Enerdynamics is an education firm dedicated to preparing energy industry employees for success in a competitive environment. We offer an array of public and in-house educational opportunities including classroom seminars, online seminars, books, and our newsletter *The Energy Insider*. We can be contacted at 415-777-1007 or info@enerdynamics.com.

Please visit our website at www.enerdynamics.com <http://www.enerdynamics.com/>

About the Authors

Bob Shively has over twenty years of experience in the gas and electric industries. As a partner in Enerdynamics, Bob has advised and educated some of the largest energy industry participants on issues ranging from market strategies to industry restructuring. Bob has also served as Vice-President of eServices of Sixth Dimension, Inc., an energy networking company, where he worked closely with retail marketing and ESCO companies in development of new economic demand response and distributed generation products. Bob began his career in the energy industry at Pacific Gas and Electric Company (PG&E). At PG&E Bob held various positions including Major Account Executive to some of PG&E,s largest end-use customers and Director of Gas Services Marketing where he was responsible for product development and sales for the company's $1.5 billion dollar Canadian pipeline project. Bob has Master of Science degrees in both Mechanical and Civil Engineering from Stanford University and is a frequent energy industry speaker

John Ferrare has worked in the energy industry as a marketing and communications specialist for over fifteen years. He began his career with Pacific Gas and Electric Company where he was integral in developing the marketing group for the company's Gas Services Marketing Department. Since that time, he has also worked with PG&E Corporation and PG&E Energy Services in the development of marketing and communication strategies. In 1995, John joined Enerdynamics to manage its educational services. In this role, he has helped create a comprehensive program to educate 600 utility employees on the changes brought by recent deregulation as well as the core classes currently offered by Enerdynamics. A graduate of Northwestern University's School of Speech, John has also developed and teaches a public speaking and communications class for a variety of corporate audiences.

ISBN 0-9741744-0-8

Edition 3.0

The authors of this book wish to thank Christina McKenna, Belinda Petty and Jack Tindall for the immeasurable improvements they suggested in reviewing drafts. We wish also to thank the thousands of participants in Enerdynamics' seminars and programs, who in the last ten years have taught the authors more than we could ever have imagined. We wish to thank the analysts at the Energy Information Administration whose data is used throughout our book. And Jeff Giniewicz whose layout and illustrations bring considerable life and vitality to our book.

Bob thanks his children Jed and Tarah for being so impressed that Dad was writing a book (although they were a bit disappointed to find out that it didn't have to do with dinosaurs or robots) and with Carol for understanding where he was the many nights spent writing. And John thanks Jesse who made sure he ate and lived in a clean house the many months that were spent writing and rewriting this book.

i

CONTENTS

What you will learn:

- The general dynamics of today's gas marketplace

- How natural gas was discovered

- How natural gas has been used since its discovery

- The technological developments that have enabled widespread use of natural gas in our society

1

SECTION ONE: INTRODUCTION

Today's Gas Marketplace

A global marketplace driving the world economy. Frenzied trading floors and frantic commodity dealers. Prices rising as demand climbs and traditional sources of supply decline. Cutthroat competition resulting in bankruptcies, business failures and wild price swings. A rapidly changing market driven by the latest technological innovations.

For many of us, such images typify the New York Stock Exchange, the oil industry and other volatile and dynamic industries. But did you know that each of these images equally applies to today's natural gas industry? In fact, the North American natural gas industry over the past several decades has transformed itself from a stodgy, blue-chip business into an exciting and competitive commodity marketplace that is now preparing to join a newly globalized gas marketplace. As little as 30 years ago this industry was subject to price regulation from wellhead to burnertip. Since then, deregulation efforts by both federal and state regulators – prodded by the entrepreneurial efforts of many market participants – have opened up the natural gas industry to the rewards and pitfalls of intense competition. By most accounts the results have been positive. According to one study (by the Energy Information Administration), the average total delivered cost of gas fell 32% for residential customers and 57% for industrial customers in the first 15 years of deregulation!

At the same time, developments in the electronic measurement and computer industries have allowed real-time measurement of gas deliveries and provided a platform for real-time trading. The result is an exciting new industry characterized by free market enterprise, competition and continual innovation. Are we nearing the end of this market evolution? Not likely! Analysts predict continued change that may ultimately lead to nationwide deregulation at the retail level. Imagine shopping for your energy provider on your home computer. Better yet, picture the convenience of choosing a provider who bundles gas, electricity, phone, cable, and high-speed internet access in one bill that arrives in your e-mail in-box and is paid by automatic debit from your checking account. Or how about moving into a new home and buying five years' worth of "comfort" credits? Your "comfort provider" guarantees the temperature in your house will remain between 70 and 74 degrees and installs everything necessary to ensure that it is – including an energy efficient furnace, air conditioner and glazed windows. You don't pay for the appliances, or even the utility bill associated with your comfort because it was all included with the service you bought.

In this book, we'll take an in-depth look at this fast-paced industry. We'll begin with a bit of history and a look at those who use natural gas. From there, we'll consider the physical system that delivers gas to end users and how the system is operated. Then on to the delivery chain and the service options available in today's marketplace. From there we'll explore regulation and deregulation and how the gas industry has evolved over the past 30 years. Then a look at the dynamics of the market and how participants make money in it. And finally, we'll get out the crystal ball and see what exciting changes lie ahead.

As you may already know, the natural gas business is filled with acronyms and industry-specific jargon which will be important for you to understand. For this reason, we suggest you begin your study with a look at the glossary and the list of acronyms found at the end of this book. We also suggest you refer back to the glossary whenever you find a word you don't understand. Once you are comfortable with these terms, feel free to study the information contained in this book in any order that makes sense for you. Good luck and have fun!

A Brief History of Natural Gas

As long ago as 1000 BC the Greeks are credited with the discovery of natural gas. According to legend, a goat herdsman was startled by what he called a "burning spring." In actuality, lightning had ignited natural gas that was seeping from the ground, resulting in an Olympic torch of sorts. Not recognizing the potential of this natural phenomenon, the Greeks proclaimed it divine and a temple was built on the spot to the Oracle of Delphi.

While the Greeks did not originally appreciate the energy potential from these burning springs, it was the Chinese who soon did. Not long after the temple was constructed at the Oracle of Delphi, the Chinese were building the first crude gas pipelines. These were constructed from bamboo poles and were used to transport natural gas for the evaporation of salt from sea water. It is believed by some that the wells that produced this gas were as deep as 2,000 feet!

In the late 1700s and early 1800s, the beginnings of the gas industry emerged in Europe. Lighting was the primary use for natural gas during this period, fueled by "manufactured gas" (produced by burning coal in a closed furnace). The heat from the burning coal drove the gas out of the furnace where it was then captured and transported via wooden pipes to these early end users. Unfortunately, this process was both expensive and hazardous to the environment.

Meanwhile, on the other side of the Atlantic, gas lighting was first introduced into the natural history museum of Philadelphia's Independence Hall in the early 19th century. And in 1816, manufactured natural gas was piped through a gas distribution system in the city of Baltimore to fuel gas street lamps. Natural gas was not used for many purposes other than lighting at this time because of the difficulty involved in transporting it to the homes and businesses where it could be consumed.

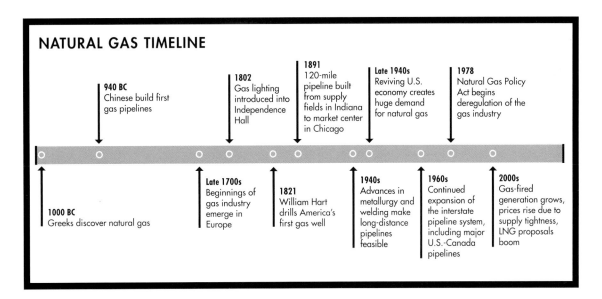

NATURAL GAS TIMELINE

940 BC
Chinese build first gas pipelines

1802
Gas lighting introduced into Independence Hall

1891
120-mile pipeline built from supply fields in Indiana to market center in Chicago

Late 1940s
Reviving U.S. economy creates huge demand for natural gas

1978
Natural Gas Policy Act begins deregulation of the gas industry

1000 BC
Greeks discover natural gas

Late 1700s
Beginnings of gas industry emerge in Europe

1821
William Hart drills America's first gas well

1940s
Advances in metallurgy and welding make long-distance pipelines feasible

1960s
Continued expansion of the interstate pipeline system, including major U.S.-Canada pipelines

2000s
Gas-fired generation grows, prices rise due to supply tightness, LNG proposals boom

A few years later, residents of Fredonia, New York noticed gas bubbles on the surface of a nearby creek. To tap into this reservoir, a gunsmith named William Hart drilled a 27 foot hole, covered it with a large barrel and piped the gas to nearby homes. This tiny, primitive contraption was America's first natural gas well, and the beginnings of the robust industry we know today. Ultimately, the Fredonia Gas and Light Company was born of this discovery – the nation's first natural gas company.

Ironically, most of the natural gas discovered during this time was regarded as a nuisance because it interfered with the original intent of the well which was to access water or brine. For the booming oil industry, natural gas was equally an unwelcome by-product of the drilling process. Gas wells discovered during the search for oil were routinely allowed to flow for months while oilmen waited for oil to appear. And gas that was produced as a by-product of petroleum drilling was often flared – a worthless hindrance because, unlike oil, it had to be piped to be of any use.

While natural gas was consumed for nearly the entire century, it wasn't until 1891 that the nation saw its first significant natural gas pipeline. This pipeline was 120 miles long and carried gas from supply fields in central Indiana to the booming metropolis of Chicago, Illinois. Amazingly, this first pipeline used no artificial compression, but relied completely on the natural underground pressure of 525 pounds per square inch (psi). As you might imagine, this and other primitive pipelines were not terribly efficient. And without adequate technology for seamlessly joining sections of pipe, or for maintaining the quality of the pipe itself, the industry did not develop extensively until the 1920s and later. During the Second World War years, advances in metallurgy and welding finally made delivery of natural gas to areas of consumption feasible. Thousands of miles of pipe were constructed and the nation saw the beginnings of an extensive and efficient natural gas delivery system.

The advancements in this technology were ultimately responsible for the natural gas industry as we know it today. As long-distance transmission of natural gas became possible, the cost of the commodity dropped, making it competitive for the first time with other fuels. Now a profitable industry, gas was used for space heating as well as lighting. After World War II, the nation's reviving economy created a huge demand for natural gas and the transmission industry boomed. This was fueled by demand for natural gas for manufacturing, cooling and refrigeration – and even electric power generation.

Since the 1960s, we have seen continued expansion of the interstate pipeline system including major projects to bring low-cost Canadian gas into the U.S. This, coupled with regulatory changes that eased restrictions on the transport of natural gas, has resulted in an integrated natural gas grid across Canada and the United States. We've also seen huge advancements in the exploration and production industry resulting in more efficient and cost-effective drilling. Most recently, the industry has benefited from a large increase in construction of gas-fired electric generation, thanks to natural gas' reputation as the cleanest burning fossil fuel. This has resulted in significant convergence between the natural gas and electricity industries as well as increased

1

demand for natural gas – a demand that is projected to grow well into the 21st century. And while demand grows, the traditional resource base appears to be shrinking, intensifying the need to access non-traditional and new resources. It now appears likely that the future belongs to a global gas business driven by increasingly large international pipeline projects and liquefied natural gas (LNG) supplies shipped worldwide.

What you will learn:

- What natural gas is

- Where natural gas is found

- What resources, reserves and supply regions are

- Where gas supply serving the United States and Canada comes from

- How resources are discovered and brought to market

2

SECTION TWO: WHAT IS NATURAL GAS AND WHERE DOES IT COME FROM?

Raw natural gas is composed primarily of methane, the simplest hydrocarbon, along with heavier and more complex hydrocarbons such as ethane, propane, butane, and pentane. In addition, natural gas typically contains non-flammable components such as nitrogen, carbon dioxide, and water vapor and may contain hydrogen sulfide which must be removed for safety and to ensure clean emissions. What we burn in our homes and offices, however, is primarily a blend of methane and ethane.

Natural gas is one of the cleanest commercial fuels available since it produces only carbon dioxide, water vapor and a small amount of nitrogen oxides when burned. Unlike the combustion of other fossil fuels, natural gas combustion does not produce ash residues or sulfur dioxides. Natural gas is often referred to as a "bridge fuel," meaning that it is the most environmentally benign energy source widely available until we further develop our renewable energy sources.

How Did Natural Gas Develop?

While several theories exist to explain the development of natural gas, the most widely accepted holds that natural gas and crude oil are the result of the decomposition of plants and animals buried deep beneath the surface of the earth. The theory goes something like this. Organic material typically oxidizes as it decomposes. Some organic material, however, was either buried before it decomposed or deposited in oxygen-free water, thereby preventing the oxidation process. Over millions of years, sand, mud and other sediments – along with these decomposed plants and animals – were compacted into rock. As layer upon layer of material covered this rock, the weight of the earth above along with the earth's heat changed the organic material into oil and gas. Over thousands of years the earth's pressure pushed these substances upward through permeable material until they reached a layer of impermeable rock where they became trapped.

Natural gas accumulates in reservoirs that are typically found between 3,000 and 25,000 feet below the earth's surface. Natural gas reservoirs are usually geologic traps in which an impermeable rock traps gas that has collected in a permeable material. When water is present in the formation, the lighter gas will displace the water to the bottom of the permeable layer. Natural gas is typically found in sandstone beds and carbonate rock, and to a lesser extent coal seams and shale beds. Wells are drilled into these reservoirs and natural gas flows upward from the high-pressure condition in the buried reservoir to the lower pressure condition at the wellhead (the top of the well at the surface). The illustration below shows the underground formations most likely to contain natural gas.

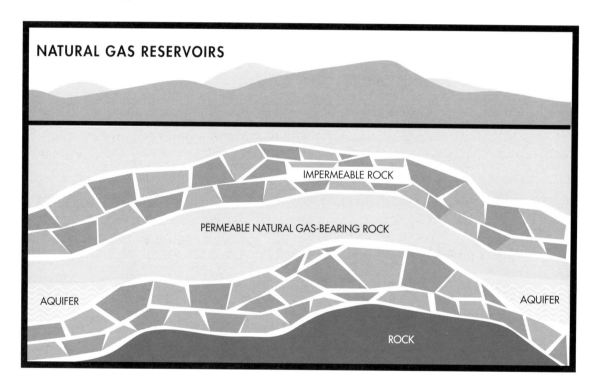

NATURAL GAS RESERVOIRS

IMPERMEABLE ROCK

PERMEABLE NATURAL GAS-BEARING ROCK

AQUIFER

AQUIFER

ROCK

Resources

Natural gas resources are quantities of natural gas, discovered or undiscovered, that can reasonably be expected to exist in subsurface accumulations. Resources may or may not have been proven to exist by drilling. Unlike reserves (which we will discuss shortly), the resource estimations are independent of factors such as accessibility, economics or technology. Categories of resources include:

2

- Proved resources — Resources that are known to exist and that are recoverable under current conditions (these are also known as reserves), plus proved amounts of gas that are currently inaccessible, uneconomic, or technically impossible to produce.

- Unproved resources — Resources that are estimated to exist based on analyses of the size and characteristics of existing fields and supply basins, but have not been proved to exist through actual drilling.

- Undiscovered resources — Resources that are generally believed to exist in fields that have yet to be discovered.

Reserves

Natural gas reserves (sometimes called "proved reserves of natural gas") refer to estimated quantities of natural gas that are recoverable in future years from known reservoirs under existing accessibility, economic and technical conditions. Reserves are considered to be proved if economic producibility is supported by actual production or test drilling of the reservoir's geologic formation. Areas of a reservoir considered to be proved include portions that have been shown by drilling to contain recoverable gas as well as immediately adjacent portions that are believed to be recoverable based on geologic and engineering data.

Gas Supply Regions

Gas reserves are located in areas called gas supply regions. The major regions supplying the U.S. include the Gulf Coast, Permian, San Juan, Rocky Mountain, Mid-Continent, Pacific Coast, and Eastern in the U.S. and the Western Canada and Scotian Shelf in Canada. The largest producing regions currently are, in order, the Gulf Coast, Western Canada, Permian, San Juan, and the Rockies. The onshore Gulf Coast, Permian, Mid-Continent, Pacific Coast, and Eastern regions are more mature supply sources, meaning that most of the easy-to-find or produce gas has already been exploited. Regions with more recent development and significant undeveloped gas resources include offshore Gulf of Mexico, San Juan, the Rockies, Western Canada, and the Scotian Shelf. However, much of the resources in these regions require non-traditional and more expensive production techniques and may also require additional pipeline construction to bring larger volumes of gas to market. Additional significant reserves exist in northern Alaska, the MacKenzie Delta in Canada and in Mexico, but pipeline facilities do not currently exist to bring this gas to the major U.S. markets. And unfortunately, the cost of building pipelines from these areas is significant. In the

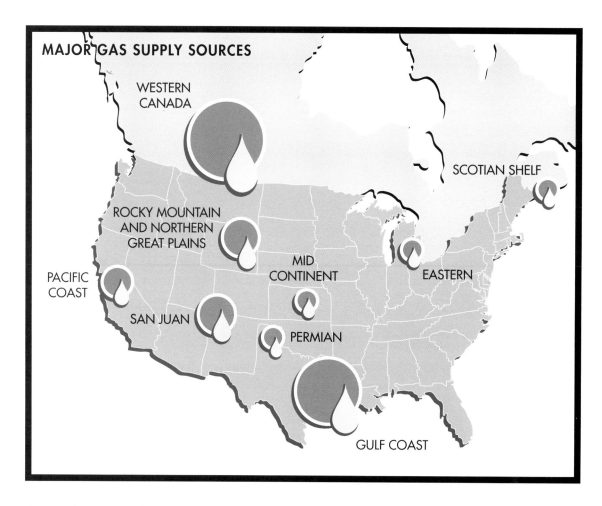

2

future the U.S. will likely depend more on natural gas from areas such as Asia, the Middle East, Russia, and South America that is transported via LNG tanker.

Gas Supply in the United States

More than 80% of the natural gas consumed in the United States is produced domestically. Much of the remaining supply is imported from Canada, with smaller but growing volumes being imported via liquefied natural gas (LNG) tankers.

In the year 2004, the U.S. consumed approximately 22.4 Tcf of natural gas. Estimates indicate that the current U.S. supply base will be insufficient to cover future needs. The Energy Information Administration (EIA) estimates that the U.S. has proven reserves of about 190 Tcf. Often, the popular press uses the consumption and reserve numbers to conclude that current reserves cover U.S. needs for less than nine years. This is, of course, a bit misleading as we are continually adding to our reserve base. It

U.S. GAS SUPPLY SOURCES (TCF)[1]

	2004	Projected 2010	Projected 2025
Consumption	22.4	25.4	29.3
Supply			
Domestic	18.9	20.4	20.8
Canada	3.2	2.6	2.6
Mexico	-0.4	-0.1	-0.3
LNG	0.6	2.5	6.4
Other[2]	0.1	0.0	-0.2
Total Supply	22.4	25.4	29.3

does, however, point out that we must continually replenish our gas resource base to keep supply in step with demand. According to the EIA, the average rate of gas production in the U.S. will increase by 0.6% per year over the next 20 years, while demand will increase by 1.6% per year. Another recent study, performed by the National Petroleum Council (NPC), forecast an even more sobering view of flat U.S. production in the future.

In recent years new supply needs have been met by increased imports from Canada. However, production from current Canadian sources is also expected to remain flat, resulting in flat or even declining Canadian imports. Even while projecting the growth of non-traditional reserves (from sources such as tight sands, coalbed methane and gas shale) and additional supplies (from remote basins in Alaska and Arctic Canada), the EIA projects that U.S./Canadian supplies will fall short by as much as 10% over the next ten years. And while significant resources do exist in Mexico, current projections suggest that Mexico will continue to use all its production domestically, thus continuing to be a net importer of U.S. supply. The forecasted supply gap will likely be filled by imports of Liquefied Natural Gas (LNG). LNG is gas that is produced elsewhere in the world, cooled below the point where it becomes

RESOURCE BASE BY REGION (TCF)[3]

	Proved	Total
Western Canada	57	224
Rockies	50	329
Gulf Coast Onshore	38	183
Gulf of Mexico Offshore	29	284
MidContinent	24	88
West Texas	16	64
Alaska	9	303

liquid, and then shipped to the U.S. via tanker ship. The EIA estimates that by 2025, over 20% of U.S. supply will be met by LNG.

Of course, a degree of uncertainty exists when trying to predict future supply/demand scenarios. Significant potential supplies exist both in the lower-48 US states, offshore

---

[1]Source: Energy Information Administration *Annual Energy Outlook 2005*.

[2]Includes net storage withdrawals and errors due to rounding.

[3]Source: National Petroleum Council.

in the Gulf of Mexico and in Alaska. One recent estimate for the total U.S. natural gas resource base showed it being as high as 2,492 Tcf[4] with an additional base of up to 465 Tcf in Canada.[5] Meanwhile the NPC estimates a total U.S. resource base of 1,451 Tcf and a base of 397 Tcf in Canada. And technological advances and development of unconventional resources such as deep gas, gas shales, deep coalbed methane, or gas hydrates could change the equation. A key question will be whether gas price levels, technology development and environmental regulations will allow these supplies to be economically produced, or whether global supplies delivered via LNG tanker will prove to be more economical.

Exploration, Drilling and Completion, and Production

The process of finding natural gas and getting it out of the ground is actually three-fold: exploration (finding natural gas and making the decision to drill for it), drilling and completion (drilling the well and equipping it for natural gas production), and production (extracting the gas and then processing it so that it's of usable quality). Let's take a look at the steps involved in bringing gas from reservoir to wellhead.

Exploration

As you might imagine, the way in which we explore for natural gas reservoirs has changed dramatically since William Hart dug America's first gas well in 1821. What began as a visual search for oil seepage in the ground or for gas bubbling under water has developed into a complex, technical and in most cases extremely expensive process. Today, the discovery of natural gas reservoirs begins with a model of the geologic formations most likely to house them. This model is then compared to a potential reservoir for similarities. Aerial photography or even satellite imaging may also be used to aid in the assessment of potential sites.

The geologist is also likely to use seismology in the search for natural gas reservoirs. Seismology (the study of how seismic waves move through the earth) enables scientists to study the lower layers of the earth's surface without actually drilling through them. Seismology gives scientists a glimpse of the various properties of the earth's layers, such as depth and thickness. This in turn enables them to determine whether such formations are likely to trap gas and oil. While the actual workings of seismic technol-

---

[4]Estimate from USGS and MMS quoted in *Outlook for Natural Gas Supply, Myths and Realities*, presented by Vello Kuuskraa to FERC, October 25, 2002.

[5]From *Canadian Natural Gas Supply/Demand Update*, October 25, 2002, presented by Craig Stringham, Canadian Association of Petroleum Producers, to FERC.

ogy are complex, a simple explanation is as follows. Intense sound waves – created by explosives or strong vibrations – are aimed at the geologic area to be studied. Sensors on the earth's surface record how these waves are reflected back to the surface by the rock below. Interpretation of these signals gives us an idea of what that formation looks like. Additional data may be collected by measuring the variations in the earth's magnetic and gravitational fields.

The most accurate method of analyzing potential resources is to drill exploratory wells. As the well is drilled, logging tests allow geologists to map subsurface formations. A series of exploratory wells allows geologists to gain a picture of the likelihood of gas throughout an area. Unfortunately, as we will see, exploratory wells can be expensive.

One of the most promising technological advances in the exploration of natural gas is 3-D seismology. 3-D seismology allows scientists to create a detailed three-dimensional map that can quite accurately predict the possibility of the existence of oil and gas in a specific location (imagine a CAT scan of the earth). Such technology has both increased our access to natural gas reserves as well as lowered the price to tap them. It has also enabled producers to return to previously drilled areas to find additional reserves that were unidentifiable with older technology.

Drilling and Completion

Once we have enough evidence to indicate the existence of a natural gas reservoir, a decision must be made on whether the economic characteristics of the reservoir make it profitable to drill a well. But before any drilling takes place, an E&P firm must first lease or purchase mineral rights and obtain the necessary permits – a process that may require extensive environmental impact studies. Once this process is complete, an exploratory well is drilled and producers do a lot of hoping and praying! Even the best technological advances cannot guarantee that natural gas will be where they think it is. In fact over 60% of exploratory wells are dry, meaning no economic amounts of gas exist. Certainly not the most favorable odds for a well which could cost as much as $15 million to drill and develop.

The placement of the exploratory well will depend on physical characteristics of the reservoir and the surface terrain, availability of gathering pipelines, as well as legal and regulatory issues such as permits. Drilling itself is performed by driving a rotating metal bit through the ground (known as rotary drilling). Offshore drilling uses similar technology but is somewhat more complicated because a platform must be constructed to hold the drilling rig. Once the drill comes in contact with natural gas, the E&P firm can begin to estimate the ultimate productivity of the new well. Hopefully the exploratory well will indicate the producers have tapped an economic resource that can be developed to a productive state.

Recent advancements in directional drilling and horizontal wells have allowed production from some formations that previously were uneconomic. Down-hole motors are used to drive the drill bit making both horizontal and multilateral wells possible. Horizontal wells pass through more of the reservoir, markedly increasing the production rate. Multilateral wells allow many reservoirs to be drilled through the same well bore. These techniques reduce the surface footprint such that one drilling location may now replace 10-15 wells drilled vertically. This can be especially important in environmentally sensitive areas or where access is limited.

Once it is determined that a proved resource exists, the next step is to complete the well so that the natural gas can safely flow to the surface. This process is called well completion. First, steel casing is cemented into the hole to prevent it from collapsing and to keep fluids from flowing through the well bore and into another formation. This is especially important in preventing fresh water contamination. Next, the casing is perforated next to the gas-bearing formation. Then production tubing is run inside the casing and attached to the wellhead. The wellhead consists of a series of valves at the surface of the well that regulate gas pressure and prevent leakage. If the gas reservoir has enough pressure and permeability, natural gas will flow to the surface naturally due to the pressure differential. In some cases, treatments are used to increase natural gas production rates. An example of well treatment is hydraulic fracturing, which is the injection of water into the well to open up cracks within the underground formation. After water has opened a crack, a solid material like sand or beads is injected to prop the crack open. These cracks allow the gas to flow to the surface more easily.

Production

Once the well is completed, equipment is installed to meter the flow of gas. Engineers then monitor the flow rate and the pressure to evaluate the effectiveness of the completion. They also use this information to forecast future production rates and the amount of gas that can be recovered from the well.

After the natural flow has been established to the satisfaction of the engineer, the next step in production is to install piping to move the gas on each individual lease to a lease facility. At these facilities, condensate and water are separated from the gas.

Condensate is an oil-like hydrocarbon that is in a vapor or gaseous state at reservoir temperature and pressure, but is a liquid at surface temperature and pressure. Condensate is sold separately. The last production function is to meter the gas going off the lease as a basis for compensating individual lease participants and royalty owners. From the lease facilities, the gas enters the gathering pipeline and is moved to a processing facility. These steps are discussed in Section Four.

What you will learn:

- Customer segments that use natural gas

- How much gas is used by each customer segment

- What uses each customer segment has for natural gas

- How usage patterns vary throughout the year

- The needs of each customer segment and the gas services they purchase to meet those needs

3

3

SECTION THREE: END USERS

All business starts with the customer, and the gas business is no exception. So before we go any further, let's take a moment to look at the various kinds of gas customers (or end users as they are typically referred to in the industry). Traditionally, end users were categorized according to the rate classes they were placed in by their local distribution companies. These included residential, commercial, industrial, and electric generation. They were placed into these customer classes because they were similarly situated (i.e., their uses for natural gas and consumption patterns were generally the same), and the regulated utility structure generally holds that similarly situated customers should pay similar rates. The chart below illustrates annual usage by each of these customer classes.

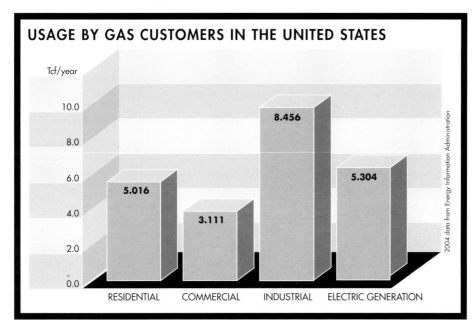

While many LDC still view customers according to these ratepayer classes, most other industry participants do not. They segregate their markets according to location, consumption patterns and specific needs, and then set out to develop products and services carefully designed to meet these criteria. For the sake of simplicity, however, we will examine end users according to traditional customer class.

As you can see from the chart on page 18, the number of residential customers far exceeds the number of commercial customers, which in turn far exceeds the number of industrial customers. Yet at the same time the industrial class uses far more gas than either the commercial or residential class. This distinction is the primary reason industrial customers tend to have far more clout both in the regulatory/political arena and in the marketplace. In fact, this political power was instrumental in initiating deregulation of the gas industry, which has resulted

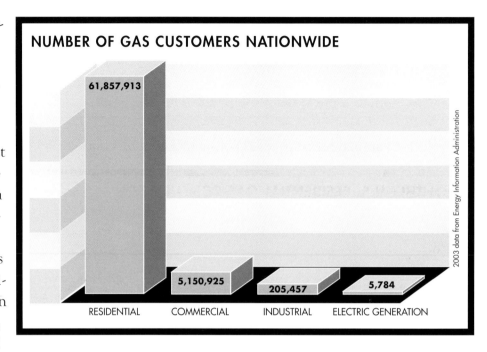

NUMBER OF GAS CUSTOMERS NATIONWIDE

61,857,913

5,150,925

205,457

5,784

RESIDENTIAL COMMERCIAL INDUSTRIAL ELECTRIC GENERATION

2003 data from Energy Information Administration

in greater benefits for industrial customers than for any other customer group. And, as markets deregulated and new products and services were developed, marketers have targeted the industrial customers first since they represent large sales volumes with limited numbers of buyers. (This is important because the cost to sell to this group is much lower per MMBtu than other groups.) Despite the initial focus on industrial benefits, many believe that ultimately deregulation helps all customers as competition results in lower cost structures throughout the industry.

In the next sections we'll take an in-depth look at the four primary natural gas end user categories. We'll find out who they are, how they use natural gas, which services they choose to buy, from whom they buy them, and how much they can expect to pay for those services.

Residential Customers

Over 60 million residential customers – comprised of single-family homes and multi-family units – utilize natural gas to satisfy one or more energy need. As we saw earlier, residential usage accounts for approximately 23% of overall U.S. usage, and has increased by an average of 1% per year over recent years – a trend that is expected to continue[1]. Reasons for an increase in residential usage include larger average size single-family homes and greater use of natural gas for space heating and gas-fueled fire-

---

[1]Usage and price data in this Section is taken from various reports by the EIA.

places. However, improvements in furnace efficiencies and building insulation effectiveness have kept this increase from being more significant.

Typical residential uses for natural gas include space heating, hot water heating, cooking, clothes drying, pool heating, and gas fireplaces. Due to the high use of natural gas for space heating, residential usage tends to peak in the colder winter months. In fact, 70% of annual residential gas consumption occurs during the months of November through March and frequently exceeds industrial consumption during these months. Residential gas consumption is very weather sensitive, and can vary by +/– 20% if the weather is colder or warmer than average.

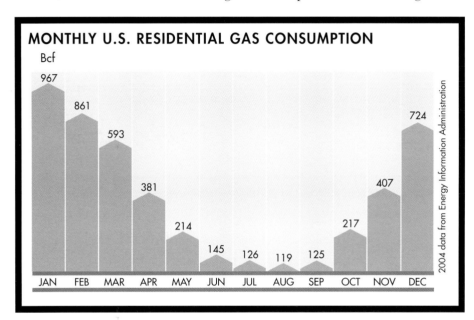

Residential customers do not generally alter usage in response to price increases since readily available alternatives do not exist once a furnace or other gas appliance has been installed in a home. The only short-term demand responses available to customers are minor such as lowering the thermostat, better insulating doors and windows or drying clothes on a clothesline. This lack of demand response is exacerbated by the fact that most gas utilities average gas prices over the year, thus failing to send clear price signals to residential customers.[2]

Key residential customer needs include:

- Gas supply on demand — Residential customers must have supply when they need it since their main uses for natural gas are for critical functions such as heating and cooking.

- Low prices — During winter months, the cost of heating can become an important factor in customers' budgets.

---

[2]Some utilities even offer payment plans that average monthly bills over the course of a year, even further insulating consumers from the realities of fluctuating gas prices.

- Stable prices — The reality of the natural gas market is that pricing can change significantly within short periods of time. In areas where regulators have experimented with a closer tie between wholesale and retail prices or where deregulation has resulted in retail market-based prices, customers have been shocked and burdened by significant monthly price volatility.

- Safety — Natural gas can be explosive and is highly dangerous if leaks occur.

- Behind-the-meter — Residential customers typically require only appliance maintenance and repair.

NATURAL GAS UNITS

Natural gas is generally measured in one of two ways – by volume or by energy content. Gas is metered based on volume. Units typically used are cubic feet (cf), thousands of cubic feet (Mcf) and millions of cubic feet (MMcf). But because the energy content (or heating value) of natural gas can vary, a more accurate way of measuring the ultimate value of gas is to use units based on energy content. (For example, you would need less cf of higher heating value gas for a hot shower, and conversely, more cf of lower heating value gas for the same shower.) Units commonly used include British Thermal Units (Btu), millions of btus (MMBtu), therms (equal to 100,000 Btu), and decatherms (equal to 10 therms).

To convert volumetric units to units based on energy content, you must know the heating value of that specific gas. The heating value tells you how many MMBtus are contained in each Mcf. A common heating value is 1.015 MMBtu/Mcf. Pipelines and LDCs meter gas based on volume, but then use meter factors based on average heating value to convert usage to energy content. They then bill their customers based on the energy content delivered.

In almost all of the United States, residential customers receive natural gas as a regulated, bundled service from their local gas distribution company (LDC). By bundled service we mean that gas distribution, gas commodity and other customer service functions are all included in one service provided by the LDC. A few states have implemented residential gas deregulation that allows residential customers to buy their natural gas commodity from retail marketing companies while continuing to take distribution service from the LDC (similar to buying long-distance phone service from Sprint while paying your local phone provider for the connection to your house). Whether or not deregulation of gas supply services has occurred, residential customers depend on their LDC to ensure service safety and for rapid response to any reports of leaks. Behind-the-meter services are generally provided by local HVAC (heating, ventilating and air conditioning) firms.

Residential customers typically pay significantly more for natural gas service than other customer groups. There are three primary reasons for this. First, the distribution system required to serve residential customers is more expensive since services are delivered in smaller quantities. Second, the high seasonal swing in usage means that much of the infrastructure – built to service the demand peak – sits idle during the rest of the year. And third, the winter demand peak tends to correspond to the highest gas prices in the year, so the costs of acquiring supply to serve residential customers are greater than the supply costs for other customer classes. For the calendar year 2004, residential customers paid an average price of $10.74/MMBtu (compared to $9.26 for commercial customers, $6.41 for industrial customers and $6.09 for electric generation customers).

The future growth of gas services for residential customers appears uncertain at best. Due to their lack of size (individually), the seasonality of demand and typical insensitivity to price, residential gas customers do not make an attractive market for new services. However, in areas where deregulation has resulted in supply choice, some large market players have begun experimenting with business models built on providing these services. In other countries such as Great Britain, where gas supply has been more fully deregulated, virtually all residential customers take gas supply from retail gas marketers rather than the LDC. In these markets, retail marketers often create additional services as a means of attracting customers and enhancing profits.

Commercial Customers

Approximately five million commercial customers use natural gas in the U.S. Typical commercial gas customers include retail establishments, restaurants, motels and hotels, healthcare facilities, office buildings, and government agencies. This customer segment accounts for approximately 14% of total U.S. gas usage. Commercial gas use has increased by an average of about of 2.7% per year since 1986. This is largely driven by an overall increase in commercial square footage, though greater usage of gas for cooling and cogeneration have also contributed. Growth in usage by commercial customers is expected to slow to 1.2% per year over the next twenty years.

Typical commercial uses for natural gas include space heating, water heating, cooking, other process heat, and cooling. Of course, it is important to realize that different commercial customers will use natural gas in very different ways. Like residential gas use, commercial gas use tends to peak in the winter due to space heating. However, seasonal consumption increases are not as dramatic as we saw with the residential sector since commercial customers also use substantial quantities of gas for process needs such as cooking, drying and cogeneration. Moreover, gas-fueled cooling adds loads in the summer. Thus, the increase in winter consumption due to colder than normal weather would typically be less than 15%.

Commercial consumption is generally driven by weather and business activity (e.g., declines in commercial business activity result in decreased consumption). Like residential customers, short-term demand response to price is

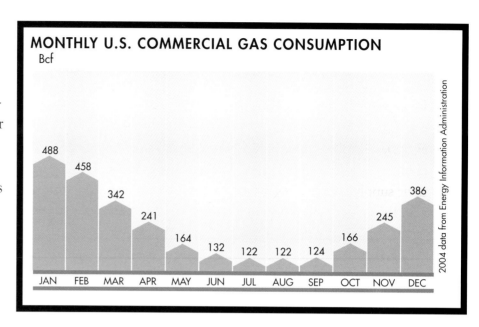

MONTHLY U.S. COMMERCIAL GAS CONSUMPTION
Bcf

488 458 342 241 164 132 122 122 124 166 245 386

JAN FEB MAR APR MAY JUN JUL AUG SEP OCT NOV DEC

2004 data from Energy Information Administration

limited, though commercial customers are more likely to track budgets for gas spending and to take actions to reduce consumption if costs exceed budgetary expectations.

3 Key commercial customer needs include:

• Gas supply on demand — Commercial customers generally consider their gas uses to be critical to the operation of their business.

• Low prices — For many commercial businesses the cost of natural gas is an important budget item.

• Stable prices — Again, utilities have traditionally hidden wholesale market price fluctuations from commercial customers by averaging prices over the course of a year. In areas where regulators have experimented with a closer tie between wholesale and retail prices, or where deregulation has resulted in market-based prices, some commercial customers may be unable to handle monthly price volatility due to cash flow issues. This concern is likely to vary significantly by business type and the extent to which the cost of their total finished product or service is attributable to natural gas.

• Safety — Natural gas can be explosive, and is highly dangerous if leaks occur. Since commercial customers are not only worried about personal safety, but also about liability for accidents, safety is a significant concern.

• Behind-the-meter — Like residential customers, commercial customers may also require appliance maintenance and repair. Since appliances tend to be sophisticated and critical to the business process, this service is often highly important for this sector. If their usage is significant, these customers may also be willing to pay for energy efficiency enhancements.

In most of the United States, access to competitive gas supply is split for the commercial sector. Commercial customers such as hotels, large office buildings, government agencies, and hospitals are often large enough to qualify for direct access to supply choice under local public utility commission rules. These customers will likely buy their supply from a gas marketer while continuing to pay their LDC for gas distribution services. Smaller commercial customers, however, are generally treated similar to residential customers and buy their supply and distribution in a bundled service. Behind-the-meter services are generally provided by HVAC firms and/or energy service companies (ESCOs). In some commercial sectors, gas marketing firms have begun to offer behind-the-meter services in addition to commodity sales.

Commercial customers typically pay the second highest cost for natural gas among customer groups. Reasons for this are similar to those listed for the residential sector (greater use of the distribution system, high seasonal load swings and winter peaks in usage). While U.S. commercial customers paid an average of $9.26/MMBtu in 2004, it should be noted that in many areas there are different rate structures and supply pricing strategies for various commercial customers. This results in larger customers paying much less than the overall group average.

Many industry participants expect that the future growth of services for commercial customers will be robust. This is primarily due to two factors: commercial customers who are likely to commit to services that will improve their bottom line profitability are not likely to have in-house expertise in these areas, and for commercial customers who are part of national chains, the wide distribution of energy efficiency strategies and/or aggregation of buying services are natural fits. Services that may come to dominate the commercial marketplace include continuous improvement in energy efficiency, sophisticated energy monitoring and consumption analysis, appliance maintenance and repair, equipment financing, supply pricing options, supply price risk management, supply aggregation, and total energy outsourcing.

Industrial Customers

Although the industrial sector includes just over 200,000 customers, it makes up almost 38% of the gas usage in the U.S. Industrial consumption grew steadily from

1986 to 1996 at an average annual rate of 4.6%. However in the late nineties, industrial gas consumption began to level off and even showed slight decreases as new capital investment in energy efficient equipment and a shift to less energy-intensive industries changed the industrial picture. Consumption spiked to an all time annual usage high of 8,142 Bcf in the year 2000 before again declining in 2001 as the economic downturn hit the U.S. Industrial demand growth is forecast to remain modest over the next twenty years, at about 1.2% a year.

Industrial uses for gas vary greatly by customer type. Significant users of natural gas include the pulp and paper, metals, chemicals and petroleum refining, stone, clay and glass, and food processing industries. Uses for gas include waste treatment and incineration, metal melting, glass melting, food processing, drying and dehumidification, heating and cooling, and cogeneration. Natural gas may also be used as a feedstock for the manufacturing of products such as fertilizers, chemicals and pharmaceuticals.

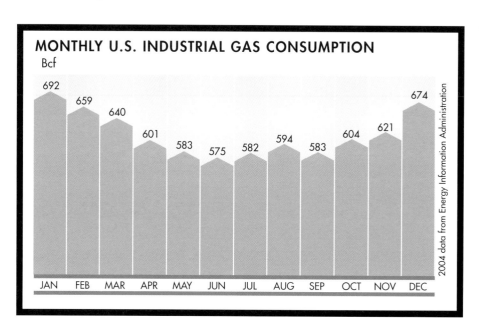

MONTHLY U.S. INDUSTRIAL GAS CONSUMPTION
Bcf

JAN 692, FEB 659, MAR 640, APR 601, MAY 583, JUN 575, JUL 582, AUG 594, SEP 583, OCT 604, NOV 621, DEC 674

2004 data from Energy Information Administration

Industrial gas use has historically been more volatile than the residential or commercial sectors. Industrial demand tends to rise and fall, with business cycles heavily impacting this customer segment. For example, industrial demand in 2002 was 13% lower than demand in 2000. Unlike residential and commercial demand patterns, seasonal fluctuations in industrial usage are minimal. In recent years, winter peak month usage has averaged only about 12% higher than the average monthly industrial usage.

While industrial demand is generally driven by business cycles, there is some demand response to price. Unlike residential and smaller commercial customers, industrial customers typically pay market-based prices for natural gas supply since their supply services are competitive in virtually all regions. Approximately one-third of industrial customers have the option to switch to alternate fuels such as propane or fuel oil. Those without fuel-switching capabilities may very well shut down production during times of high prices, either because they can make higher profits by re-selling gas they had already purchased than they could by manufacturing, or because the high cost of gas makes their facilities no longer economic to run. Global manufacturers may also have the option of shifting manufacturing to other countries where fuel prices are lower.

Key industrial customer gas needs include:

- Gas supply on demand — Although industrial customers were once classified as "noncore" by utilities (i.e., their supplies could be interrupted during times of high demand), since the advent of deregulation and service by marketers rather than utilities, industrial customers now expect their supplies to be available whenever they are needed.

- Low prices — For many industrial businesses the cost of natural gas is a large budget item, in some cases as much as $1 million per month.

- Stable prices — Stable pricing is critical for many industrial customers. Since gas often makes up a significant component of their variable cost of production, profit margins may be dependent on meeting or beating budgeted energy costs. Thus many industrial customers are very interested in securing fixed gas pricing – either paying a margin to reduce the risk of price volatility or participating directly in financial markets to hedge commodity price risk.

- Safety — While safety is of primary concern, many industrial customers have their own maintenance staff, so they are less concerned with receiving services relating to safety on their own premises.

- Behind-the-meter — Industrial customers tend to have their own facilities engineering and maintenance staff and pay careful attention to equipment efficiency since this is a primary driver of their cost structure. Industrial customers are also likely to view this function as a core competence and are less likely to depend on outside providers for these services. However, they may benefit from certain specialized services that do not fit within their traditional areas of expertise (examples are monitoring and analysis of energy usage at multiple points throughout their facilities or analysis of employee behaviors to reduce energy consumption).

- Marketer-type services — Some industrial customers use enough gas that they have their own gas buyers on staff. In such cases, these buyers assume many of the functions normally handled by gas marketers. These companies may also directly purchase services offered by interstate pipelines and/or storage companies such as balancing, peak-day storage, long-term storage, and other hub services.

In almost all of the United States, industrial customers have the option to purchase their gas supply from retail marketers. In many cases, industrial customers are served directly off interstate pipelines and completely bypass LDC service. In cases where service directly from an interstate pipeline is not available, industrial customers pay the LDC for transport service. Because many industrial customers have alternatives to LDC service (alternate fuels or building their own connection to the interstate transmission line) and the costs to serve them are low, LDC rates are usually significantly lower for industrial customers than for commercial or residential customers. In 2004, U.S. industrial customers paid an average price of $6.41/MMBtu for natural gas, about 60% the average residential price.

While industrial customers are attractive to suppliers thanks to their large steady loads, profit margins are lower since industrial customers typically have numerous options for purchasing their gas supplies. And opportunities for additional margins through sale of value-added services may be limited since many industrial customers maintain such expertise in-house. Recent services have focused more on risk management or provision of total energy needs on an outsourced basis. This business has recently taken a setback due to the decline of many large energy marketing companies. Whether new providers will come into the market to offer these services in a reliable way remains to be seen.

Electric Generation Customers

There are currently over 5,000 gas-fired electric generation units in the U.S. (this number does not include cogeneration units located at industrial or commercial end-use customer sites). Electric generation usage in 2004 accounted for approximately 25% of total U.S. usage.

Natural gas usage by electric generation units was relatively stable during the 1980s and early 1990s. Beginning in 1996, however, electric deregulation drove the construction of significant new gas-fired generation, and consumption for this sector grew by an average of almost 11% per year through 2000. Growth was due both to higher electricity demand and to increased usage of natural gas generation as more efficient gas units were brought on-line. Beginning in 2001, a decline in electricity demand (due to the slowed U.S. economy, cooler weather and greater availability of hydro power in the California market) coupled with rising gas prices brought an end to the huge growth in gas demand for electric genera-tion – at least for the interim.

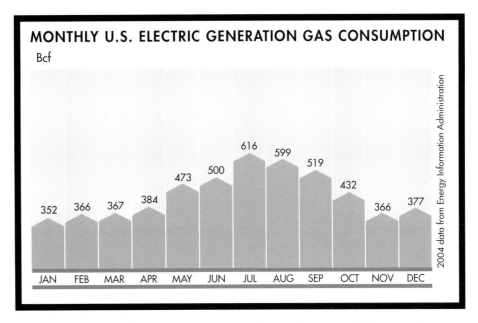

MONTHLY U.S. ELECTRIC GENERATION GAS CONSUMPTION
Bcf

JAN 352 FEB 366 MAR 367 APR 384 MAY 473 JUN 500 JUL 616 AUG 599 SEP 519 OCT 432 NOV 366 DEC 377

2004 data from Energy Information Administration

Despite the current down-turn, the future is likely to see greater gas usage for this sector. Electric generation gas demand is expected to continue increasing with an average annual growth rate of 3% over the next twenty years. Some projections show gas usage for electric generation exceeding gas usage for industrial purposes by the year 2020.

Natural gas is used by electric generators in two ways – as the fuel burned to create steam to run a steam turbine, or as a primary fuel for a gas turbine.

Seasonal fluctuations in gas usage for electric generation are substantial. However, unlike residential and commercial usage which peaks in winter, gas consumption for electric generation peaks in the summer in most regions of the country. This is due to the high demand created by air conditioning. In recent years, summer peak month usage has averaged about 50% higher than monthly average electric generation usage.

As we have seen, electric generation demand for gas can also be highly variable from year-to-year, driven by the demand for electricity, the cost of natural gas, weather, and the availability of hydro power. It is not uncommon for electric generation gas demand to fluctuate by as much as 15% from year-to-year based on these variables.

Key electric generation customer gas needs include:

• Gas supply on demand — Gas units are typically used to meet intermediate and peak demand. Additionally, gas-fired units are often used for system reserves, meaning that these units must have the ability to come on quickly should other supply sources become unavailable to meet demand. In extreme cases, units may need to go from stand-by to full generation in as little as ten minutes. So electric generation must have gas available quickly and whenever market or system conditions require units to run.

- Low prices — In a competitive electric market, gas-fired generation units will only run when the variable cost of generation with gas is lower than the market price for electricity. Since as much as 80% of the variable cost of generation for a gas unit is determined by the price of gas, low price is a primary driver in choosing to run these units.

- Stable prices — Stable pricing is critical for gas generators to make long-term plans. For new units, financing of construction costs is often conditioned upon securing a long-term commitment for stable gas prices. So it's not surprising that generating companies are frequent users of either long-term fixed price contracts or of financial instruments designed to lock in long-term gas price levels.

- Safety — While safety is of primary concern, all electric generating units have their own maintenance staff and are less concerned with receiving services relating to safety on their own premises.

- Behind-the-meter — Virtually all electric generating units handle behind-the-meter functions internally and do not require external services for this function.

- Marketer-type services — Many electric generation facilities are either owned or run by generating companies or utilities. In such cases, internal buyers take on most of the functions normally handled by gas marketers. Thus these companies may directly utilize services offered by interstate pipelines and or storage companies such as balancing, peak-day storage, long-term storage, and other hub services.

In almost all of the United States, electric generation customers purchase their gas supply from competitive marketers or directly from gas producers. In many cases, electric generation customers are served directly off interstate pipelines and do not take service from the local LDC. In cases where direct service from an interstate pipeline is not available, electric generation customers pay the LDC for transport service. Because electric generation customers are highly price-sensitive and the cost to serve them is usually low, LDC rates are significantly lower for electric generation customers than for commercial or residential customers. Electric generation customers also pay the lowest average natural gas price of all customer classes thanks to the large volumes they consume – and to the fact that their summer demand occurs at a time when demand from other customers is at its lowest. In 2004, U.S. electric generation customers paid an average price of $6.09/MMBtu.

While electric generation customers are attractive to suppliers from the standpoint of requiring huge amounts of supply, profit margins again are low since these customers are likely to have numerous options for gas purchasing. An additional risk factor is the volatility in usage – natural gas units may not be economic in the marketplace or may not be needed due to low electric demands. Thus natural gas units tend to be served either by large marketers who can handle the risk or by integrated energy marketers that are naturally hedged by being involved in both gas and electric markets. Some integrated marketing companies have offered services called tolling, where the marketers provide gas supply and market the unit's electricity output. This allows operators of units to focus on a core competence of operating generating units. Opportunities for traditional value-added services appear slim in this sector.

What you will learn:

- How gas is gathered and processed

- How gas is transported from wellhead to consumer

- How gas travels through a high pressure transmission line

- How gas travels through a distribution system

- How gas is stored

4

SECTION FOUR: THE PHYSICAL SYSTEM

Now that you understand the various end user groups and their specific needs, let's turn our attention to the physical system that was constructed to deliver gas to them. You will learn later in this book that use of the physical system has changed dramatically over the past few decades. Yet the general structure of the delivery system itself has changed little since natural gas was introduced into the United States over a century ago:

- Underground natural gas reservoirs are discovered through exploration.

- Natural gas is produced from wells that remove the gas from reservoirs.

- The raw gas is gathered by a system of small pipes and delivered to a lease facility where it is separated from production liquids.

- Gas is then moved in a gathering system from multiple leases or fields to a processing facility that removes impurities.

- The gas enters a mainline pipeline system for transportation to a local distribution system.

- Either the pipeline, the distribution system or a storage facility stores the gas until it is needed.

- And finally, the local distribution system transports the gas to end-use locations where it is consumed.

In this section, we'll study the physical side of the natural gas business. In doing so, we'll follow the steps a molecule of natural gas takes on its journey from wellhead to the burnertip.

Gathering and Processing

After it is produced at the well, gas is moved to lease facilities where it is metered to allow royalties to be paid to each leaseholder. From the lease facilities, gas is transported through a small pipeline called a gathering system. A typical gathering system may

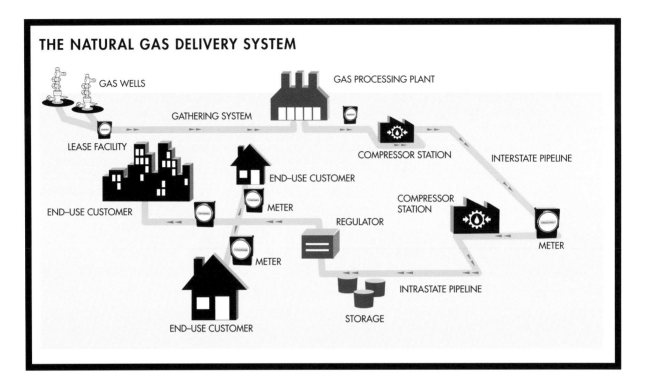

THE NATURAL GAS DELIVERY SYSTEM

GAS WELLS

GAS PROCESSING PLANT

GATHERING SYSTEM

LEASE FACILITY

COMPRESSOR STATION

INTERSTATE PIPELINE

END-USE CUSTOMER

END-USE CUSTOMER

METER

COMPRESSOR STATION

REGULATOR

METER

METER

INTRASTATE PIPELINE

END-USE CUSTOMER

STORAGE

4

link scores of individual lease holdings or multiple fields through hundreds of miles of gathering lines. Gathering systems employ smaller pipes than transmission systems because there are smaller quantities of gas to transport. Operating pressure for a gathering system can vary considerably depending on the pressure of the gas produced from the wells. If necessary, compressors are used to boost the pressure to meet transmission pipeline inlets.

Raw gas from the various lease facilities is transported through the gathering system to a processing facility where it is separated into flammable gases and liquids (methane/natural gas, ethane, propane, butane, and pentane) and nonflammable gases (carbon dioxide and nitrogen), and impurities such as water vapor, sulphur, and solids (sand) are removed if the quantities of these materials exceed pipeline standards. The natural gas liquids (ethane, propane, butane, and pentane), often called NGLs, are valuable by-products of the processing and in some situations are worth as much as the natural gas. Other by-products such as sulphur and carbon dioxide may also be processed and sold. Processing facilities are usually located on the gathering systems so that the gas is processed and cleaned prior to entering a transmission line. Less frequently, gas is processed directly at the wellhead. It may also be reprocessed on the mainline pipe to further extract NGLs. If the gas contains significant amounts of condensate (gas that becomes liquid when exposed to atmospheric pressure), the condensate is removed early in the flow process and is sold like crude oil.

Transmission

The transmission system is responsible for moving large quantities of gas over long distances (from supply basins to consuming regions). Transmission systems typically operate at pressures between 600 and 1,200 psi (pounds per square inch). Key components of the transmission system include the pipe, compressor stations, valves, and metering equipment. The volume of gas that a pipeline can transport is determined by the diameter of the pipe, the maximum allowable operating pressure (MAOP) rating of the pipe, the location of compressor stations, the amount of compression at each station, and ambient conditions such as temperature and elevation.

Transmission line pipe is typically 24 to 36 inches in diameter and constructed of .25" to .75" thick steel. Laterals off the main pipe may be constructed of smaller 6 to 16 inch diameter pipe to provide service to LDC systems or directly to large end-use customers. The pipe is coated with a specialized fusion bond epoxy coating to prevent corrosion.

As gas enters a transmission system it must be pressurized to match the higher pressure of the system. This is achieved through the use of compressors, which are contained within a compressor station. A typical compressor station includes one or more centrifugal compressors that use a fan to squeeze or compress the gas. As the gas is compressed, its pressure rises, thus forcing the gas into the pipe at the outlet and driving the gas down the pipeline. Centrifugal compressors are driven by the drive shaft of either a gas turbine or an electric motor. If a gas turbine is used, gas from the stream flowing in the pipeline will be used to drive the turbine. An alternate compressor technology is a reciprocating engine. This engine, similar to the engine used in your car, is also powered by natural gas and drives the compressor drive shaft. In addition to the compressor technology, compressor stations also generally include scrubbers and filters (to capture any liquids or solid particles that have condensed out of the gas stream during transport), monitoring probes for the SCADA system, and bypass piping and valves that allow the gas to be routed around the station if compression is not required or if maintenance is being performed at the station. Compressor stations are generally located 50 to 100 miles apart on the pipeline.

Because gas moves from areas of high pressure to areas of low pressure, the gas is pushed away from the high pressure of the compressor station to downstream areas where the pressure is lower. As gas flows through the pipe, pressure drops due to friction with the pipe walls. When the pressure gets too low to maintain an effective rate of flow, more compression is used to force the gas molecules together, again propelling them through the transmission line. This process is repeated until the gas reaches a distribution system or end user. Because gas that is under greater pressure

---

HOW LINE PIPE IS CONSTRUCTED

The pipe used in transporting natural gas is constructed in either of two ways. For the larger pipe that is predominantly used on the transmission system, a mill manufactures a steel plate that is formed into a cylindrical shape. A seam is then welded and tested using ultrasonic and/or radiological equipment to withstand pressures well beyond those for which it is designed. For the smaller line pipe typically used on a gathering or distribution system, a mill produces a cylindrical bar of steel that is pierced to create a hole through which the gas will flow. This technique is used to create pipe with diameters ranging from 0.5" to 24". Regardless of the technique used to create the pipe, all steel line pipe is coated to protect it from corrosion and other damage.

---

moves more quickly and takes up less space, pipeline companies are often able to increase the capacity of their systems by adding compression rather than actual pipe.

4

For obvious reasons, it is important for the pipeline company to always know how much gas is in its system as well as how much gas is delivered to downstream pipelines. To ensure this, metering stations are installed at various locations, typically wherever gas enters or leaves the system. Since gas meters measure volume of flow (Mcf) and gas is often traded based on energy content (Btu), calorimeters must be used at various locations on the system to determine heating value (the amount of Btus per Mcf). A metering station may also contain pressure regulation equipment to ensure that gas leaving or entering the system does so within a specific pressure range. This is important for the safe operation of the transmission system as well as the gathering or distribution systems connected to it.

It is also important for a pipeline company to monitor the many miles of pipe that comprise its transmission system. Supervisory Control and Data Acquisition (SCADA) systems automatically monitor the operations of the system. Information such as flow volumes, pressures and temperature is transmitted via a variety of communication devices to the pipeline's Gas Control room, many hundreds or even thousands of miles away. From this room, Gas Control personnel are able to monitor and control many of the pipeline's operations.

DISTRIBUTION LINE PIPE

Line pipe on the distribution system is comprised of five types of piping:

Supply main — This is the pipe that runs between the interconnection with the transmission system and the actual distribution system. It operates at a pressure between the two systems, and might also be used to provide a direct connection from the transmission system to a large industrial customer.

Feeder main — This is the pipe that connects the supply main (at the regulator) to the distribution main.

Distribution main — This is the pipe that snakes throughout the service territory bringing gas to areas of mass consumption.

Service line — This is the much smaller line that connects your home or business with the distribution main that may be running underneath your street or sidewalk. These lines are typically owned and maintained by the utility.

Fuel line — The final connection to your appliances, the fuel line is anything beyond the LDC meter that runs into your home or office. This is owned and maintained by the property owner.

One way that Gas Control regulates the flow of gas on the pipeline is through use of mainline valves. These valves, which are installed anywhere from five to 20 miles apart, enable the pipeline to isolate an area of pipe in the event of an emergency or the need for pipeline maintenance, or to restrict flows to reduce volumes based on operational or market needs. If, for instance, the pipeline were to seriously rupture, the SCADA equipment would quickly report the situation to Gas Control. Gas Control would then shut the closest valves on either side of the rupture to isolate the leakage of gas. This might be done remotely or manually. Once the trapped gas had been vented, maintenance personnel could safely repair the pipe. Unfortunately, SCADA equipment is not sensitive enough to detect all problems with the pipeline, so operators must also rely on visual inspection of the system.

Gas moves relatively slowly on a transmission line, typically from 15 to 30 miles per hour. In fact, it can take several days for a molecule of gas to travel from wellhead to burnertip (compared with electricity which travels at the speed of light!). When the gas arrives at the citygate (the intersection between the mainline transmission and the distribution system, operated by the local distribution company), the pressure is reduced and the gas enters smaller distribution pipes for ultimate delivery to end users. There are currently over 300,000 miles of main transmission lines in operation in the United States.

Since gas pipelines operate at high pressures, leaks can result in serious accidents. Thus, pipeline companies have rigorous safety and maintenance procedures that include SCADA monitoring, aerial patrols, periodic pipe inspection, pipeline markers, and emergency response teams. Pipeline safety is regulated by the U.S. Department of Transportation.

Distribution

Distribution systems are joined to transmission pipelines at an interconnect. At the interconnect are meters, regulators to depressure the gas, and scrubbers and filters to ensure the gas is clean and free of water vapor. Also at the interconnect, the distribution company will inject mercaptan into the gas. Mercaptan is a harmless odorant that has the familiar smell of rotten eggs we all associate with natural gas. Because natural gas has no natural odor, this odorant is added before the gas enters the distribution system so that gas can be detected in the event of a leak.

Natural gas is delivered from the transmission system to end-use customers by the distribution system. Unlike the transmission system, which carries large volumes of natural gas at high pressures, the distribution system winds through cities and other areas of gas demand at much lower pressures and through much smaller line pipe – typically from two to 24 inches in diameter. Pressures range from 60 psi (nearer the transmission line) to 1/4 psi as it reaches a home or small business. This pressure is important because the appliances used in your home or business were not designed to accommodate high gas pressure. Thus, as a rule, the closer the pipe gets to the end user, the smaller it is and the lower the pressure gets.

While most residential and small commercial customers accept gas service at 1/4 psi, some larger industrial and commercial customers may operate machinery that requires a higher pressure. Regardless of the ultimate delivery pressure, regulators are used to drop the pressures on the system to acceptable levels for the various end-use customers who take service from the distribution system.

Distribution systems consist of pipe (also called mains and lines – see box on page 35), small compressors that are used to boost pressure, regulators that are used to reduce pressure, valves that are used to control flow, metering used to measure flow at each customer location, and a SCADA system that provides the capability to monitor and sometimes remotely control components of the distribution system.

In many areas, plastic or PVC is now used for the construction of new distribution lines. Unlike the steel used for mainline transmission, PVC is flexible, corrosion-resistant and costs less to install. Interestingly, a recent gas replacement project in San Francisco discovered distribution pipe made of redwood dating back to the early 1900s!

There are over one million miles of distribution pipe in operation in the United States today. As you might imagine, maintaining this massive amount of pipe is difficult but essential. Distribution pipe is inspected regularly to ensure it remains leak-free. LDCs employ extremely sensitive leak detection technology both above and below ground to survey their pipelines. Distribution companies also sponsor public education programs to encourage the public to promptly report suspected leaks and always maintain 24-hour service crews to respond to any reported leak. Leaks in a distribution line are repaired in a similar manner to those found on the transmission line, with valves on either side isolating the leak.

Storage

Natural gas is stored because demand and pricing for gas varies over time (from hour-to-hour, day-to-day, and season-to-season), because it is more efficient to produce and transport gas at a relatively consistent level rather than according to the specific demand at any given moment, and so that market area demand peaks can be met even when transportation capacity is inadequate to serve peak demands. Essentially, storing gas enables market demand to be met without dramatically altering production and transportation levels. Longer-term storage is available through underground facilities, while shorter-term storage is often achieved through line pack (holding gas within the system's pipes).

HOW UNDERGROUND STORAGE WORKS

Natural gas on the surface is pressurized so that it can be injected into the underground storage facility. If a reservoir is being used, the gas will occupy the same geologic formations it occupied prior to being produced. As the gas is injected, the pressure inside the reservoir (or other suitable formation) increases. When it's time to withdraw the gas, the field operator opens valves to allow the gas to flow to the surface. The accumulated pressure acts in much the same way as a new discovery, pushing the gas toward the lower pressure on the surface.

A certain quantity of "cushion" gas is required for the gas to be withdrawn from the storage facility. This gas is not withdrawn during the process, but stays in the reservoir to provide enough pressure for the withdrawal gas to flow. "Working" gas, in contrast to cushion gas, is the gas that is injected and withdrawn – or cycled – during the storage cycle.

Underground storage facilities may be located at either the production area (production-side storage) or near the citygate (market-area storage). This longer-term storage is provided by injecting gas into underground formations when it is not required by the market, and subsequently withdrawing it when there is market demand. Most gas storage facilities are located underground, commonly in depleted gas or oil reservoirs, aquifers or underground caverns such as salt domes. Depleted reservoirs are most common because they often already have production equipment in place and are proven to be efficient storage facilities.

Traditionally, gas was injected into storage facilities in the summer months when usage was lowest, and withdrawn during the winter months when usage was highest. In other words, gas was cycled on a yearly basis. This traditional storage cycle also allowed storage users to take advantage of pricing differentials because gas historically has been cheaper during the summer months. However, with the increased use of natural gas for electric generation purposes, storage is now cycled throughout the year – both to meet peak demand and to take advantage of pricing differentials. The U.S. currently has 415 underground natural gas storage sites with a working gas capacity of 3,923 Bcf and a daily deliverability of 78 Bcf.

4

In areas where underground storage is not available, LDCs use LNG storage and propane-air peak shaving plants to provide gas to meet peak needs. LNG facilities cool and liquefy natural gas that is stored at near atmospheric pressure in large tanks with a double wall design similar to a large thermos. When peak supplies are needed, the gas is warmed, converted to vapor and then returned to the natural gas pipeline network. A propane-air system takes advantage of the fact that propane, when combined with the right mixture of air, burns similarly to natural gas. In the propane-air system, liquid propane is stored in tanks. When peak supplies are required, the propane is heated to the boiling point in a vaporizer, blended with air to create the right burning characteristics, pressurized to pipe pressures, and injected into the distribution system.

As we saw earlier, short-term storage can also be provided by holding an inventory of gas within the system's pipes. Gas system operators use line pack as a means of balancing the system or meeting customer demand even if supply delivered to the system on a given day does not match consumption. Line packing is an opportunity for short-term storage that was once available without charge to gas customers. Customers would simply nominate more gas into the system than they expected to use on a given day, then take it out of "storage" on another day when usage was greater than the supply nominated. Because the use of storage has changed so dramatically in the last decade, such free storage is not as easily obtained! Pipelines now often charge for this service.

LNG – AN ALTERNATE DELIVERY SYSTEM

In 2004, 97% of the gas supply in the U.S. was delivered from the supply basin by pipeline. An alternative to delivery by pipeline is to convert the gas to LNG and ship it in a tanker. Natural gas can be converted to liquid by cooling it below approximately -260 degrees Fahrenheit. After the conversion, the volume is reduced by a factor of 610, making it practical to transport by tanker. Because large volumes of LNG can be moved across long distances where pipelines are not feasible, LNG makes it possible for North America to access natural gas reserves that are located throughout the world.

The LNG delivery chain consists of gas production, gas liquefaction and processing, shipping, and regasification. After the gas is produced, it is shipped by pipeline to a gas liquefaction facility that cools the gas to convert it to liquid. The facility also performs any necessary processing. After liquefaction, the LNG is pumped into tankers and transported across the ocean to the consuming country. There the tanker pumps the LNG into tanks where it is stored until needed. The LNG is subsequently regasified by heating and can then be transported by pipeline to the distribution system. After regasification, the natural gas has properties similar to other gas in the pipeline system.

As gas supplies in North America become more difficult and expensive to exploit, it is expected that LNG will play an increasingly important role in North America's supply portfolio. The amount of natural gas reserves worldwide is huge. Current reserves are estimated to be 180 Tcf, which is equivalent to almost 70 years' worth of gas at current world consumption rates. It is estimated that LNG can be produced, liquefied, shipped, and regasified at a cost of about $4/MMBtu, which is significantly lower than current market prices in North America.

What you will learn:

- How the physical system is operated

- The functions of various Operations groups

- The nominations, scheduling and allocation process

- How Gas Operations runs the system on a day-to-day basis

- What curtailments and flow orders are, and when they are required

- What balancing is and how it works

- How the role of system operations has evolved

5

SECTION FIVE: GAS SYSTEM OPERATIONS

Now that we've seen the process by which natural gas is produced, transported and delivered, let's take a look at how the physical system is operated. As you know, natural gas flows through a system of pipes, compressors, regulators, and valves for final delivery to end-use customers. Day-to-day management of this system is the responsibility of the pipeline's Operations Department. Both interstate pipelines and LDCs have Operations Departments that operate their respective systems based on models of how the system will run under given conditions, information about existing and expected conditions, the volumes of gas nominated by customers, demand expected from end-use customers, and the volumes of gas injected or withdrawn from storage.

The continuing evolution of the gas market and entry of new market players has placed increasing demands on gas operations. Sophisticated information systems and flexible operating policies are now necessary to satisfy customers whose needs are becoming increasingly complex. For anyone involved with either side of a gas transaction, an understanding of the physical capabilities and limitations of the system is critical. This section provides a general overview of how the system operates, how gas is scheduled on the pipeline and the LDC, and how it is ultimately delivered to end-use customers.

Gas Planning

Gas Planning is responsible for modeling the gas system to predict how it will operate under a specific set of conditions. These models are necessary for both long-term and short-term forecasts. Long-term forecasts are used to determine what facilities need to be installed and/or overhauled on a system to meet future gas demand. Short-term forecasts are also necessary to determine daily system demand and capacity given specific conditions such as time of year, temperature, compressor availability, price differentials, and storage operations. The results of the model are used by Gas Control to make important day-to-day operating calculations such as the volume of gas the pipeline can accommodate on a given day and whether or not this volume will be adequate to meet expected demand.

Pipeline Operations

As described above, the pipeline Operations Department will manage the pipeline system on a day-to-day basis based on physical conditions and forecasts of expected needs for gas along the system. Gas Control is the central command center responsible for operations and safety of the pipeline system as a

---

MAKING A NOMINATION

A nomination is simply a request to move gas from one location to another. It is typically made 24 to 48 hours prior to the day of gas flow and indicates points of receipt and delivery (commonly an interconnect with an interstate pipeline and an end-use location), the contract number under which the gas is to flow on the pipeline on which it was nominated, and the contract number on which the gas is to flow for the upstream (and if appropriate the downstream) pipeline. Once it receives the nomination, the scheduling group confirms the upstream source and the downstream recipient to ensure that the nomination matches gas that the pipeline will receive from or deliver to other pipelines. Gas Scheduling also checks the availability of capacity to ensure that all nominations will be able to flow. If demand for service at a specific point exceeds capacity, allocation procedures are used to schedule the nominations and certain nominations are trimmed. After all gas has been scheduled, nominations are confirmed back to customers via daily scheduling reports.

---

whole. To perform this function, Gas Control continually views data collected remotely from across the pipeline system and then communicates operational requirements to Field Operations. Field Operations performs any functions that cannot be performed remotely by Gas Control as well as necessary maintenance on the system.

Gas Scheduling – Pipeline

Gas Scheduling provides the link between customer demand and Gas Control's operation of the system. It is the role of Gas Scheduling to receive nominations for gas onto the system and schedule them according to the pipeline's various rules of operation. If nominations exceed system capacity, they are scheduled based on the priority rules set forth in the pipeline's tariffs. Schedulers on interconnected pipelines and interconnected storage fields must also work together on a daily basis to determine how much gas can flow, and then to track ownership of the gas as it moves from one system to the next.

As you might expect, scheduling gas on a pipeline is a complex task. In the past, when only a few parties held contracts to move gas, nominations were made with a paper nomination form and a fax machine. In today's marketplace, with literally hundreds of entities owning space on a pipeline, nominations are made via internet access to a pipeline's nomination system. Complexity in scheduling has also increased in recent

WHAT IS THE NAESB AND WHAT WAS GISB?

As electronic nominations and movement of gas across an interconnected grid became the industry norm, the need arose for standardization between the various interconnecting pipelines. This is especially important since marketers often need to move gas across several pipelines, with widely varying rules and procedures. For instance, nominations might be due at noon on a downstream pipeline, yet not due upstream until 5 p.m., meaning that you would need to nominate gas before knowing whether there was capacity available upstream. Out of this confusion was born the Gas Industry Standards Board, or GISB (pronounced "gis-bee"). GISB was a voluntary organization whose mission was to develop and maintain standards for business transactions in the gas industry. The goal of GISB was to increase the efficiency of the natural gas system in the U.S., thereby making natural gas a more attractive competitor in the marketplace. The efforts of GISB have done a lot to further the development of a national pipeline grid that is well integrated across multiple pipelines and numerous market participants. On January 1, 2002, GISB was absorbed into a new organization, the North American Energy Standards Board (NAESB). NAESB is designed to expand the role that GISB played in the gas industry to provide standards for both gas and electric industries.

years as pipelines now accept and process nomination throughout the gas day rather than once daily, which was the norm a few years back.

Pipeline Allocation

At various peak periods, a pipeline system cannot physically accept and deliver all the gas that customers have nominated. When this happens, the pipeline must allocate the available space according to predetermined allocation policies. Pipelines generally have two levels of priority: firm and interruptible. Firm customers are always scheduled first, followed by interruptible. If all firm nominations cannot be accommodated, they are generally reduced pro-rata (i.e. everyone's nomination is reduced by the same percentage) to the capacity available on that day. Interruptible nominations are often scheduled based on price paid since interruptible service is frequently discounted. Allocation rules for pipelines are spelled out in the pipeline's tariffs.

LDC Operations

Much like the pipeline Operations Department, the LDC Operations Department manages the distribution system on a day-to-day basis based on physical conditions and expectations of end-use customer needs. Again, Gas Control is the central command center responsible for operations and safety of the distribution system. Gas Control continually views data collected remotely from across the distribution system and is also tied directly into the customer services center that will receive any calls concerning gas leaks. Gas Control communicates operation requirements to Field

Operations which performs any functions that cannot be performed remotely as well as any necessary system maintenance.

Gas Scheduling – LDC

Unlike pipeline schedulers who have a primary goal of fulfilling firm customers' nominations and maximizing pipeline throughput, LDC schedulers are most concerned with ensuring all customers have adequate supply to fulfill their end-use demands. Thus, LDC schedulers generally schedule flows based on expected deliveries from upstream pipelines and/or local storage facilities and on forecasts of expected customer usage. It is the scheduler's job to schedule the LDC system so that enough gas is available in the pipeline at a high enough pressure for all end-use customers to be able to use the amount of gas they desire (while, of course, maintaining the safety and integrity of the system). If gas deliveries do not match forecast demand, schedulers may meet demands by drawing from line pack, withdrawing gas from storage or, as a last resort, imposing flow orders or curtailments. Like pipeline scheduling, LDC scheduling has become increasing complex with the evolution of the gas industry. At one time, schedulers simply managed the gas utility's own sources of supply and storage. Now schedulers must juggle deliveries from numerous marketers and independent storage fields, as well as downstream fluctuations from huge power plants who are ramping up and down hourly based on electric market conditions.

Curtailments and Flow Orders

When usage is at its greatest, deliveries into the LDC are short, or there is a physical problem with the LDC system, Gas Control may be required to take steps to ensure system integrity. The first step is to require end-use customers to match their usage to the quantity of gas they deliver onto the LDC system on a given day. This requirement is generally called an Operational Flow Order (OFO) or Emergency Flow Order (EFO), although LDCs in different parts of the country may use slightly different terminology.

Flow orders may be used when there is too much gas coming into the system, resulting in over-pressurized pipes (a safety issue), or when there is too little gas coming into the system, resulting in loss of pressure and hence inability to get gas to end-use customers. A flow order directs certain customers to match the amount of gas they bring into the system to the amount of gas they are using on that given day. Customers who fail to match supply to usage face a penalty. Frequently, flow orders are issued in stages. An initial stage might result in a penalty of $0.25 per decatherm plus the market gas price for usage that does not match supplies. If the initial stage does not return the system to a safe operating status, flow orders are often escalated to higher penalties. Penalties on some systems can reach $50 per decatherm plus the market gas price. Generally the $50 penalty is a good incentive to halt excess usage!

If use of flow orders does not bring the LDC system back to a condition where all end-use customers can be served safely, the LDC must implement curtailments (orders to halt usage altogether). Just as with pipeline allocation, there is a specified order in which customers are served during a curtailment. But unlike pipelines, which generally allocate based on firm versus interruptible status, LDCs curtail based on customer type. Generally, electric generators, industrial and large commercial customers are curtailed first to ensure continued service to residential and small commercial customers. This is because larger customers often have alternate fuel back-up systems (propane for example) and, more importantly, because loss of natural gas service to residential customers may result in public health issues (e.g., loss of heat on a cold day). If necessary, small commercial customers will be curtailed prior to residential customers. Since it is not practical for LDCs to physically shut off gas to each large end-user, stiff penalties are put in place for any non-authorized gas usage during a curtailment. Specific rules for flow orders and curtailments are found in each LDC's tariff book.

Gas Control

You learned in the last section that the Gas Control group operates the compressors, regulators and valves to ensure that safe operating pressures are maintained on the pipeline and customer demand is met. There are four primary tasks that Gas Control must complete on a daily basis:

- System forecasts — It is crucial that the pipeline anticipate customer usage as closely as possible on a day-by-day basis. To estimate usage, Gas Control takes historical and current data (such as weather forecasts, nominations, usage forecasts, storage activity, line pack, as well as any expected maintenance on the system) and runs the model developed by Gas Planning to develop a forecast of how the system will likely be used for up to five days out. Each day this forecast is fine-tuned to get the most accurate picture of what will actually happen on gas flow day. If the forecast indicates an over or under-capacity situation, the appropriate measures will be put in place to ensure the integrity of the pipeline.

- Implementation of the plan — Next, Gas Control uses their forecast to determine how the pipeline will be used (i.e., how much gas can be scheduled, the appropriate line pack and the pressures required to run the system as planned). This information is then communicated to the various personnel responsible for running the pipeline.

- Monitoring the plan — Equally important is monitoring the pipeline to ensure that the specific planning that Gas Control has done is accurately implemented. For instance, a malfunction with part of the system or higher or lower usage than expected will alter the pipeline's plan. Gas Control must react in real-time to keep the pipeline operating smoothly.

- Recording — And finally, Gas Control must record the daily activity on the pipeline. Rarely do customers use the exact amount of gas they had anticipated. Thus it is important to maintain precise records that account for all the gas on the system.

Pipeline Maintenance

Proper maintenance of the pipeline is crucial to its smooth and dependable operation. This includes emergency repairs as well as planned maintenance. Without proper maintenance any system will eventually fail, resulting in the pipeline's inability to serve customers and quite possibly a dangerous situation. Maintenance groups use models, manufacturer's recommendations, physical monitoring, and experience of the system to plan scheduled maintenance. In determining when and how a system is repaired, planners must balance the cost of routine maintenance with the safety, cost and inconvenience of outages caused by unplanned maintenance. Planners must also balance the timing of planned outages with both customer service needs and the financial consequences of the down time.

In addition to repairs, pipelines also require routine maintenance such as internal cleaning and continual monitoring for leakage or other pipeline damage. While uncommon, the dangers of catastrophic ruptures on a mainline pipeline are familiar to all of us, and are something a pipeline wishes to avoid at all costs. While there are any number of ways to inspect and maintain a pipeline, one of the most important devices used is called a "pig." This device travels through the pipeline cleaning it of any matter that may have adhered to the inside of the pipe. A "smart pig" goes one step further and actually transmits data regarding the internal condition of the pipeline back to the pipeline operator.

Balancing

Users of natural gas are
rarely able to forecast exactly how much gas they will
need on a given day.
Product rates go up and
down, weather affects cooling and heating loads, and
power plants may be run or
shut down depending on
electric loads. Thus it is rare
that actual gas through the
meter on any given day
matches the amount nomi-
nated. Similarly, producers
and interconnected
pipelines may experience
variations in day-to-day volumes from amounts forecast
or contracted for.

Balancing is a technique
used throughout the industry to allow parties to manage day-to-day fluctuations
in deliveries and/or receipts.
In the case of an end user,
balancing allows the cus-
tomer to take gas each day
matched to his actual

A BALANCING EXAMPLE

- Joe's Manufacturing nominates 100 MMBtu each day for a month.

- All nominated quantities are scheduled and received as planned from the upstream pipeline.

- But instead of the 100 MMBtu they had anticipated, Joe's uses only 80 MMBtu each day.

- By the end of the month Joe's is 600 MMBtu (20 MMBtu x 30 days) out of balance.

Since Joe's total gas usage for the month was 2,400 MMBtu (80 MMBtu x 30 days) they are more than 10% out-of-balance, the maximum typically allowed by the LDC. Thus the LDC notifies Joe's they have one month to correct the imbalance.

Joe's corrects their imbalance the next month as follows:

- They underdeliver by 10 MMBtu each day (i.e., 70 MMBtu/d) thereby reducing their imbalance to 300 MMBtu.

- Joe's is still out of balance so they find a marketer, Jill's Trading Company, which has a negative imbalance (Jill's has consumed more gas than they nominated) and they trade 300 MMBtu of imbalance between them. Now Joe's is back in balance.

Note that this example assumes monthly balancing. Many systems have moved to daily balancing (the above example should explain why!), where any imbalances greater than 10% must be corrected within days rather than at the end of the month.

demand (rather than his anticipated demand, which may be quite different) and either owe gas back to the LDC/pipeline or have gas owed to him. In the case of a producer with variable flow, balancing applies to the pipeline's receipt of supplies. Even interconnected pipelines will use balancing to handle day-to-day differences between actual physical flows and contractual flow quantities. To manage these differences, pipelines often put in place Operational Balancing Agreements (OBA) that allow them to balance their systems on an ongoing basis.

A decade ago, pipelines asked their customers to balance on a monthly basis. That is, customers would add up the total amount of gas delivered into the pipeline on their behalf along with the total amount of gas they actually used for the same period. Any imbalance could be either traded with another customer on the pipeline or cashed out by buying or selling the gas from or to the pipeline. When the gas business was simpler, monthly balancing worked just fine. However, with the proliferation of marketers and other third parties owning contracts on a pipeline system, misuse of this system became widespread. It was not long before these parties saw a way to increase their margins at the expense of the pipeline companies or other ratepayers.[1] As a result, many pipelines now ask their customers to balance on a daily basis. These pipelines offer various services to help customers deal with the inevitability of imbalances. They also retain the right to impose hefty penalties for those who are not able to keep imbalances within a pre-determined tolerance band.

LDCs still tend to utilize monthly balancing since daily balancing is viewed as overly burdensome on end-use customers. But, as described above, LDCs utilize flow orders to require daily balancing during times of system stress.

5 The Evolving Role of Operations

The simultaneous evolution of open access gas markets and information technology has significantly impacted the way the gas business is conducted and the way many pipelines operate their gas systems. Prior to deregulation, LDCs controlled the supply, storage and receipt of gas and needed only to manage their systems to meet end-use customer demand. Since numerous parties now buy gas, use storage facilities and transport gas for delivery to end users, system operation is much more complex. Forecasting demand and system needs is an increasingly difficult science. The evolution of the gas business has both necessitated and been facilitated by the development of electronic metering, electronic bulletin boards, and more sophisticated nominations systems. Consequently, it is not unusual for trading and deliveries to occur on a daily or even hourly basis. This has required Gas Operations to become a more sophisticated and continually evolving critical function of both the pipeline and the LDC.

---

[1] We have seen in earlier Sections that gas prices vary significantly, even from day-to-day. Loose balancing rules allow customers to use gas they didn't purchase on days when gas is expensive, and then pay it back on days when it's not.

What you will learn:

- The market participants in the upstream, midstream and downstream sectors

- The services offered in each market sector

6

SECTION SIX: MARKET PARTICIPANTS IN THE DELIVERY CHAIN

Not so many years back, a section on the natural gas delivery chain would have been very short. Producers produced gas and sold it to interstate pipelines. They in turn delivered it to the citygate and sold it to the LDC. And LDCs, of course, delivered and sold it to the end user. Compare that with today's gas market where a myriad of participants take on these roles: producers, aggregators, gatherers, marketers, pipelines, storage providers, hub operators, financial service companies, local distribution companies, end users, and many others. To make this structure even more complex, the distinctions between various participants often blur as companies add value to their service by playing multiple roles and rebundling services. In this section, we'll take a look at these market participants and assess the value they add to the natural gas delivery chain.

As we study the industry's market structure, we will divide these entities into three groups: upstream (generally associated with the production aspect of the industry), midstream (generally associated with the transmission aspect of the industry), and downstream (generally associated with the distribution aspect of the industry). Some participants such as financial services, marketers, integrated energy companies, and storage providers may be associated with several or all areas of the industry.

Market Participants
UPSTREAM
• Producers
• Gathering Pipelines
• Aggregators
• Financial Services Companies
MIDSTREAM
• Marketers
• Shippers
• Interstate Pipelines
• Storage Providers
• Hub Operators
• Financial Services Companies
• Electronic Trading Exchanges
DOWNSTREAM
• Local Distribution Companies
• Retail Marketers
• End Users

Upstream Participants

Producers

Natural gas producers, also known as E&P (exploration and production) firms, explore for gas reservoirs, drill wells and produce gas. Larger producers may also market their gas directly to end users. Others rely on aggregators or marketers to make the connection with end users. Because natural gas and oil are often found together, many of the largest natural gas producers are also major oil producers. Examples of influential natural gas producers are BP, ExxonMobil, Chevron, Shell, ConocoPhillips, Devon Energy, and EnCana.

Gathering Pipelines

Connecting the lease facility with the transmission system is an important function provided by the gathering pipelines. While the producers themselves may handle this function, it is often a third party who owns and operates these small, extended pipeline systems. In addition, the operators of a gathering pipeline may also operate the processing facility necessary to remove impurities from the gas stream and to strip valuable natural gas liquids. Examples of companies operating gathering pipelines are Duke Energy Field Services, Williams and Kinder Morgan.

Aggregators

Aggregators act on behalf of groups of producers to pool supplies and sell the gas in commingled blocks to end users or midstream marketers. Aggregators do not take title to the gas but simply find markets and negotiate prices for their customers. The role of the large aggregator has declined in recent years and is now generally confined to larger producers who aggregate supplies on behalf of smaller producers in a specific production region.

Financial Services Companies

In the upstream sector, financial services companies provide two important functions. First is financing E&P activities. Since almost all of the capital required to find and develop reserves is expended prior to attaining revenues for the gas, the ability to borrow money at reasonable rates is critical to E&P firms. The second function is to provide risk management services associated with gas pricing. Given the capital-intensive nature of the business, extended periods of low prices can result in severe financial difficulties for an E&P firm. Thus many firms will want to lock in guaranteed prices for at least a portion of their supply portfolio. Financial services companies offer hedging products that allow a firm to do so. Financial houses serving the industry include Morgan Stanley, Merrill Lynch, Goldman Sachs, and Citigroup.

Midstream Participants

Marketers

Marketers generally purchase gas supplies from producers or aggregators and then resell the gas to end users, LDCs or other marketers. In some instances, marketers may also sell a specific producer's gas without taking title in return for a marketing fee. Successful marketers add value by saving producers and end users the trouble of finding each other, arranging transportation and storage, and sometimes even arranging financing or assuming price risk.

TOP NORTH AMERICAN GAS MARKETERS[1]

		Bcf/day
1.	BP	24.8
2.	Sempra	12.2
3.	ConocoPhillips	11.2
4.	Coral	10.8
5.	Atmos	6.6
6.	Cinergy	5.9
7.	Nexen	5.1
8.	Chevron	4.9
9.	Tenaska	4.1
10.	Oneok	3.6

Customer choice (meaning the customer is free to buy gas supply from someone other than the distribution utility) is currently available to almost all large commercial, industrial and electric generation customers in the United States. And in some states, customer choice is also offered to smaller customers. Thus the role of the marketer is important. During the late 1990's a number of large marketing companies emerged. Many of these encountered financial difficulties in 2001/2002 and by 2003, most of the top marketers from earlier years (including Enron, Dynegy, Mirant, Duke, AEP, and Aquila) were no longer active in the business. New companies that have filled this void include producers who directly market gas (such as BP Energy, Chevron, ConocoPhillips, EnCana, ExxonMobil, Nexen, and Shell), financial houses moving into physical marketing (such as Goldman Sachs, Louis Dreyfus, Merrill Lynch, and UBS), utility-based trading subsidiaries (such as Cinergy and Sempra), as well as smaller regional marketers.

Shippers

A shipper is any market participant holding a contract to transport gas on a pipeline or LDC. Shippers may be end users, marketers, producers, or other LDCs.

---

[1]Source: *Natural Gas Intelligence* (intelligencepress.com), numbers are for first quarter 2005.

Interstate Pipelines

Pipelines transport gas from producing regions (or supply basins) to market regions. Before FERC deregulation, pipelines also took title to the gas they transported and subsequently resold the gas to local distribution companies (LDCs) or end users. Currently, most gas transported by pipelines is owned by third parties such as marketers, producers or the end users themselves. There are literally hundreds of interstate pipelines criss-crossing the United States. Some of the largest pipelines include ANR, Transco, Texas Eastern, Northern Natural, and Columbia Gas Transmission. Pipelines tend to be owned by larger holding companies such as El Paso, Duke, Williams, MidAmerican, and Kinder Morgan.

MARKET AFFILIATE RULES
As you look at the list of top gas marketers and the list of large pipeline holding companies, you may notice that many companies appear on both lists. For obvious reasons, pipelines or utilities are not allowed to favor their own marketing companies in providing transportation or other services. Both FERC and state utility commissions vigorously enforce what are known as Market Affiliate Rules. These rules state that regulated entities must treat all customers the same and may not provide any non-public information to companies with which they have common ownership. If any employee provides information to an employee of a related company, this information must immediately be provided to all other customers. Regulators take Market Affiliate Rules very seriously and significant fines (in the many millions of dollars) have been assessed in the past to companies that have failed to follow the rules.

Storage Providers

Storage providers operate storage fields and offer storage services to a variety of market participants. Pipelines, LDCs and hub operators also provide short-term storage known as balancing and/or parking. Depending on rate methodology, balancing may be provided for a separate fee or may be bundled into transportation rates. Ownership of storage facilities is slowly moving out of the hands of pipelines and LDCs and into the hands of independent operators. Likewise, storage capacity, which was typically held by LDCs to meet seasonal periods of peak demands of their own customers, is being cycled year round and is now often held by marketers or other independent operators providing services to third parties. Examples of new independent storage operators and developers include HNG Storage, Haddington Ventures and Falcon Gas Storage.

Hub Operators

Hub operators provide various services at points where multiple pipelines intersect. These services include wheeling between pipelines, exchanges, title transfers, price discovery, electronic trading, and parking and lending. The map on page 55 shows the

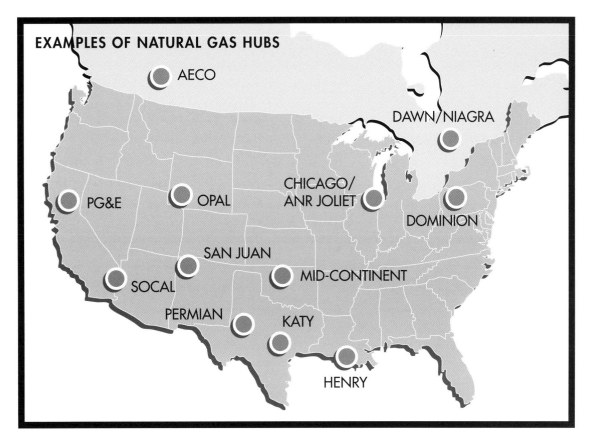

EXAMPLES OF NATURAL GAS HUBS

AECO

DAWN/NIAGRA

CHICAGO/
ANR JOLIET

PG&E   OPAL   DOMINION

SAN JUAN

SOCAL   MID-CONTINENT

PERMIAN   KATY

HENRY

locations of the major hubs throughout the United States and Canada. The largest hub in North America is Henry Hub in Louisiana, which is owned and operated by Sabine Hub Services. Examples of other hub operators include ANR Pipeline (ANR Joliet), ENSTOR (Katy Hub), EnCana (AECO Hub), Nicor Enerchange (Chicago Hub), and Pacific Gas and Electric Company (Golden Gate Market Center).

Financial Services Companies

Financial services companies assist market participants with products that help them hedge risk of price fluctuations. Many market participants do not wish or cannot tolerate the risk of price fluctuations that occur in a commodity market. For these participants, the fee charged by financial service companies is a small price to pay for insulation from market variables. Examples of financial houses serving the industry include Goldman Sachs, Louis Dreyfus, Merrill Lynch, and UBS.

Electronic Trading Exchanges

The last few years have seen the emergence of centralized electronic trading exchanges. These include the NYMEX futures exchange as well as private exchanges that provide a place for marketers and other market participants to trade commodity.

Prior to the emergence of the electronic trading exchanges virtually all trading was done by phone, and large volumes continue to be traded in this manner. Operators of electronic exchanges include the Intercontinental Exchange (ICE) and the New York Mercantile Exchange (NYMEX).

Downstream Participants

Local Distribution Companies (LDCs)

LDCs transport and distribute gas from the interstate pipeline to end users. LDCs may also take responsibility for purchasing and reselling gas to certain classes of end-use customers. Municipal utilities are entities that perform the functions of LDCs, but are owned by the municipality and are not regulated by the state utility commission as the LDCs are. Prior to deregulation most gas was purchased by LDCs and resold to end users under regulated rates and rules. Currently, many large end users – and in some states small customers – hold title to their own gas and simply pay the LDCs for transportation services. The largest LDCs in the U.S. include Southern California Gas, Pacific Gas and Electric, PSE&G, Nicor, Consumers Energy, and MichCon.

Retail Marketers

While many end-use customers simply turn to their LDC for services and information related to their usage of natural gas, larger customers are likely to require more comprehensive services. These customers may look to gas marketing companies or producers for commodity (gas sales) services and to marketers or energy services companies (ESCOs) for additional services behind-the-meter. Most large customers, and in some states even small customers, buy their gas commodity from gas marketers and simply pay the LDC for transport service. Often these companies add value to the commodity they sell by offering additional services such as energy management and conservation, energy usage analysis and facilities auditing, consolidated billing, and integrated energy (which includes gas, electricity, cogeneration and other ways of optimizing overall energy use). ESCOs offer similar services without selling commodity. Examples of active retail marketers include Direct Energy, Shell Energy Services, Coral, Constellation New Energy, and SCANA.

End Users

End users are the ultimate consumers of natural gas. They include residential, commercial, industrial, cogeneration, and electric generation customers. Residential and smaller commercial customers are classified as core customers, while the remainder are classified as noncore customers. Generally, noncore customers have alternatives to LDC services such as the ability to satisfy their energy needs with alternate fuels like propane or fuel oil. Refer to Section Three for details on various energy end users.

What you will learn:

- The services commonly offered in upstream, midstream and downstream sectors

- Who offers what services in each sector

- Characteristics of common gas services

- How contracts are used to define service terms

7

SECTION SEVEN: SERVICE OPTIONS

In the last section you learned about the various market participants involved in the natural gas value chain. In this section, we will once again follow the value chain from production to end-use consumption. This time, however, our focus will be on the various products and services available in the upstream, midstream and downstream markets.

SERVICE OPTIONS			
Sector	Services Provided	Service Providers	Service Consumers
Upstream	Gathering Processing Supply Risk Management	Pipelines, Producers Pipelines Producers Marketers, Banks	Producers Producers, Marketers Marketers Producers
Midstream	Supply Transportation Storage Hub Services Risk Management	Marketers, Producers Pipelines Pipelines, Storage Cos. Pipelines, Storage Cos. Marketers, Banks	Marketers, LDCs, End Users Producers, Marketers, LDCs, End Users Marketers, LDCs Marketers, LDCs, End Users Marketers, LDCs, End Users, Pipelines
Downstream	Supply Distribution Storage Hub Services Risk Management Behind-the-Meter	Marketers, LDCs LDCs, Pipelines Storage Cos., LDCs Storage Cos., LDCs Marketers, Banks Marketers, ESCOs	End Users, Retail Marketers End Users End Users, Retail Marketers End Users, Retail Marketers End Users, Retail Marketers End Users

Upstream Services

Gathering

Gathering services provide the necessary transportation from the producer's lease facility to an interstate pipeline. Often, a producer or a group of producers will own and operate the gathering system for their own wells, and neighboring producers may purchase transport services from them. In larger fields, gathering services may be provided by gathering pipelines owned and operated by companies that specialize in this service.

Gathering services are often not regulated and service terms are determined through negotiation. Because transport must be assured before investing in the large capital costs associated with proving a well, it is not unusual for gathering contracts to be long-term in nature and at relatively fixed prices.

Processing

Most gas that comes from wells must run through a processing facility to remove impurities and to establish the desired Btu content. These facilities are typically run by either the interstate pipeline or gathering pipelines and services are generally provided at a cost per volume. A key issue in determining pricing for processing services is who has rights to the valuable natural gas liquids extracted from the gas stream. If this right is held by the processor, they may recover much of their cost of operation from sales revenues, thus charging less for processing.

DEVELOPING A SUPPLY PORTFOLIO

A typical supply portfolio for a marketer contains an assortment of supply contracts designed to minimize risk and maximize profit. As you will see, each supply market offers benefits as well as risks to its customers. To examine how a marketer develops a supply portfolio, let's use Sally's Marketing as an example.

The long-term market is used primarily for security of both supply and price. As it turns out, Sally's has a fixed-price supply contract with all the Burger Kings in Maryland. So do you think Sally's wants to take the risk of buying gas on the daily spot market to serve this customer? Probably not. But at the same time, Sally's wants to take advantage of times when the price of gas is low. Just as an investor doesn't put all his eggs in one basket by buying only one stock, Sally's doesn't buy only long-term supply at a fixed price.

That's where Sally's spot purchases come in. Every day, Sally's traders need to buy or sell varying amounts of supply to meet their customers' demand. When the prices are down, Sally's tries to buy for days or even weeks at a time to take advantage of the savings. And when prices are high, Sally's looks to storage or other products available from the pipelines to minimize extended exposure to high prices.

Supply

Historically, gas supply in the production basin was purchased by interstate pipelines. Today, this gas is generally sold to marketers or large producers who are aggregating a supply portfolio. Buyers may also include very large end users, utilities or electric generation companies (though these represent only a small percentage of the buyers active in the production basins).

Up until the 1980s it was not unusual to see gas supply contracts for periods of ten or even thirty years. In general, deregulation has drastically reduced the willingness of market participants to enter into such long-term agreements. Today, contracts for gas supply range from one to five years (long-term), monthly or for periods less than a month. The market for such short-term purchases is called the spot market. Unlike the long-term market, the spot market can fluctuate wildly from week-to-week and even from day-to-day. So those buying gas under spot conditions assume the risk of high costs when prices rise and reap the benefits of low costs when they fall (much the same as a stock market day trader).

Pricing for supply agreements also varies widely and depends upon the needs and wants of the contracting parties. Pricing options include fixed and indexed prices, with a variety of choices in each category. Fixed pricing guarantees a specific $/MMBtu price for a specified length of time, while indexed prices are determined at specific intervals (yearly, monthly, daily) based on a published market index. A typical index price might be determined by taking the NYMEX Futures Henry Hub closing price for a month and reducing it by $0.35/MMBtu. Of course, pricing can quickly become more complex with both fixed and indexed prices included in one contract. Other key contractual parameters include whether the supply is firm or interruptible, whether the contract is for a fixed volume or for flexible volumes, and whether the buying party is obligated to purchase the gas whether or not they take delivery (this type of provision is known in the industry as "take-or-pay" but really means take it and pay – or don't take it and pay anyway!).

Risk Management

Producers and marketers holding assets or contracts that are subject to market fluctuations may turn to the financial markets to hedge a portion of the price risk. Thus there is also a market for financial risk products in the upstream sector. Common products include price swaps (exchanging variable price risk for a fixed price) and options (the ability to create price floors and ceilings to reduce risk of price fluctuation). We will take a much closer look at these concepts in a later section of this book.

Midstream Services

Once natural gas enters the interstate pipeline, market participants require services such as supply, transportation, storage, hub services, and risk management. Most of the users of midstream services are gas marketers, although large users, LDCs and electric generation companies may also be active.

Supply

Midstream supply arrangements are similar to upstream arrangements with the exception that as supply gets closer to end users, contract terms are generally shorter.

Transportation

Once a supply deal is secured, a shipper next looks for the least expensive path to get the supply from the point where it's bought to the point where it will be sold. This could involve arranging for transportation on several interstate pipeline systems.

Service Options

As with supply, numerous options now exist for interstate gas transmission. Transportation can be contracted for either long-term or short-term commitments and, on some pipelines, seasonally. Contracts are also available for firm (guaranteed) or interruptible (as the name implies, this service is never certain and can be interrupted if the space is needed by shippers with higher priority) service.

Unless there is some sort of emergency situation on the pipeline, a shipper expects that firm service will be available on every day for which it is contracted. And firm service has the highest priority of any of the services sold on a pipeline. There are a number of important terms associated with a typical firm transportation contract:

- Maximum Daily Quantity (MDQ) — This is the maximum quantity a shipper can transport over the pipeline on any given day. Because it is rare that a shipper will transport her full MDQ on every day, pricing is structured into two components:

- Demand Charge — This is an amount, based on the capacity contracted, that must be paid whether the shipper uses the capacity or not. This is also known as a "reservation charge" because it entitles the shipper to reserve space on the pipeline.

- Commodity Charge — This is an amount paid by the shipper based only on the actual capacity used on a given day.

In contrast to firm service, interruptible or "as-available" service is understood to be non-guaranteed and has a lower priority on the system. Pricing for this service is also variable (up to a tariff cap), depending very much on market conditions at the time of use. Unlike firm service, interruptible service users typically pay only a commodity charge, and are not charged an up-front fee to contract for the service. There is also no commitment to ever use the service. However, when the shipper does move gas an MDQ will apply just as for firm service. This MDQ is generally determined by the amount of credit the shipper has established with the pipeline.

Rates

Rates for transportation service vary depending on the structure used by the individual pipeline. There are generally three types of rate treatments found on U.S. pipelines: zone rates (much like many metro commuter rail systems, a user pays rates according to the number of zones crossed), postage stamp rates (as with the postal service, the price is the same no matter where you go), and mileage-based rates (the price depends on the number of miles the gas is transported). The exact rates and rate structures applicable to a specific pipeline can be found in the pipeline's tariffs, which are available to anyone who may consider using the pipeline's services and can usually be found on the pipeline's website.

Secondary Markets

FERC Order 636 (issued in 1992) authorized the sale of transportation capacity on the secondary market (known as capacity release). This enabled a capacity holder to assign on either a temporary or long-term basis any unused firm capacity. The effect of Order 636 was to establish rates more in line with the market value of the capacity. Maximum rates, however, are generally set by the regulator, so the secondary market is not yet a totally free enterprise.

Secondary transactions are posted on the pipeline's electronic bulletin board (EBB) and are subject to certain rules and regulations. Primary among these are requirements that capacity offerings be non-discriminatory, meaning that they are offered to any party willing and able to pay for them. Posting of available transportation also allows for price transparency, which is crucial for a true commodity marketplace. If a shipper is looking to permanently release capacity, it is posted on the EBB and sold to the highest bidder. While the pipeline may have certain creditworthiness requirements for a third party purchasing this transportation, any qualified buyer is entitled to all the rights and privileges of the original owner of the capacity.

Storage

With the deregulation of the gas industry and the increased use of natural gas to power electric generation, underground storage has evolved from a seasonal process to a continuous, year-round cycled service. Storage service has three components: injection (getting gas into the storage facility), inventory (the gas actually held in the storage facility over a period of time), and withdrawal (getting the gas out of the storage facility). All three services comprise a storage "cycle." Depending on the physical capabilities of the individual facilities, gas can be cycled a few or many times throughout the year to meet peak demands.

Just as with transportation, storage service is available on a firm or as-available basis. The same priority rules generally apply to these services as well. What's different is the way the service is priced. As mentioned above, the user will pay for the service in three components:

- Injection — The user will pay a variable rate in $/Dth to put gas into storage. For firm service, he may also pay a monthly demand charge.

- Inventory — Here, the user pays a reservation charge (monthly or annually) in $/Dth that entitles him to store a specific amount of gas.

- Withdrawal — Just as with injection service, the user pays a variable rate in $/Dth withdrawn. For firm service, he may also pay a monthly demand charge.

Users of storage often supplement their firm service with as-available service, which may be purchased through the storage owner or from other contractors of storage service.

Storage services are often available on both the upstream and downstream ends of pipelines. Upstream storage is often called production-area storage while downstream storage is generally called market-area storage.

Hub Services and Market Centers

A recent innovation in the pipeline business is the establishment of hubs and market centers. These entities provide a number of services including wheeling between pipelines, exchanges and title transfers, electronic trading and price discovery, and parking and lending. Following is a brief discussion of each of these services.

Wheeling

Hubs that connect multiple pipelines often transfer gas from one pipeline system to another in exchange for a small fee (often less than one cent per MMBtu). This service is known as wheeling. By contracting with the hub to handle all the mechanics of scheduling between the multiple pipes, the shipper is saved hassle and time.

Exchanges and Title Transfers

Hubs are common places for one marketer to trade gas with another. Again, shippers are often happy to have the hub handle the mechanics of the transfer for a small fee. An additional benefit is that if a marketer is transferring gas from one third-party seller to a second third-party buyer (the marketer, of course, is charging a margin on the sale), she does not want the two parties to get to know each other since next time they could cut her out of the transaction. So by paying for a blind title transfer, the marketer protects her markets.

Electronic Trading and Price Discovery

By creating a common trading point where numerous parties make transactions, price discovery can be obtained. Perfect price discovery occurs if all participants are using an open electronic exchange where aggregated data for all transactions is made public. Electronic trading can also reduce costs associated with traditional trading done over the phone. Even where electronic trading is not available or is not widely used, relatively accurate price discovery can be obtained through entities such as Bloomberg or Platts which poll traders daily to establish an index price (an estimated average transaction price at that location). Other benefits of electronic trading include standardization of contract terms, and in some cases exchange-provided insurance for counterparty risk. The marketplace is slowly moving towards widespread adoption of electronic trading.

Parking

In addition to underground storage service, pipelines are also able to offer some storage services through line pack. This service depends on the usage of the pipeline at the time this storage is requested and may not be available at all times of the year. Storage that is offered through line pack is called parking. As the name implies, the gas is "parked" on the system until a later date when it is needed. By adding more compression, pipeline operators are able to pack their system with additional gas supplies. Because the gas does not need to be injected into an underground facility, a parking transaction is generally simpler than the multiple transactions required for underground storage. As the market became more competitive, system operators realized there was a value for this short-term storage. So, when system conditions allow, pipelines are happy to offer this storage product.

Lending

Lending is the opposite of parking. Here the pipeline draws from its system inventory to offer a temporary loan of gas. Again, system operators recognize the value of this service, especially with the price swings that are typical in certain periods. Because both parking and lending affect the inventory on a pipeline system, they can only be offered when conditions allow.

Risk Management

Marketers and other shippers (producers, LDCs, or end users) as well as pipelines themselves will likely have price risk associated with their involvement in midstream markets. Thus all of these participants may turn to the financial markets to hedge a portion of this risk. Common products include price swaps and options. We will take a much closer look at these concepts in Section Eleven.

Downstream

In the traditional regulated marketplace, end users simply purchased a bundled gas product from their LDC. However, in virtually all markets in the U.S. and Canada, large end users now have the option of purchasing their supply from marketers rather than the LDC. And in areas where a large end user is located near an interstate pipeline, they will often connect directly to the interstate pipeline and bypass the LDC entirely. Such market evolution has led to an increase in services required by the downstream sector.

Supply

For customers with a choice of gas supplier, supply arrangements are generally non-regulated and are negotiated freely between buyer and supplier. End user agreements are rarely more than a year in length with the exception of some very large electric generators and/or industrial customers. Most end users prefer to sign one-year agreements, with pricing either fixed for the year or tied to a market-based index. Other key provisions include whether the contract covers all volumes required by the end user or simply a fixed volume, whether there is a minimum take-or-pay, and who is responsible for any balancing charges imposed by the LDC or pipeline.

Customers without supplier choice purchase their gas from the LDC under regulated tariffs that are set by the state public utilities commission. Pricing is generally on a volumetric basis (per MMBtu) but in some states may include a demand charge associated with maximum volumes required during the year. Pricing is often fixed for a twelve-month period or longer, but in some states may be adjusted as often as monthly based on market conditions.

Distribution

Distribution service refers to moving gas from the LDC interconnection with the interstate pipeline to the customer's facility. This service may be provided as a separate

66

unbundled service or may be bundled into the supply service. In situations where end users are buying supply from a marketer rather than the LDC, this service is often called transport service or transportation.

Rates and terms of service for distribution service are set by the state public utilities commission. Large customers often have the choice of firm or interruptible transport. Rates for firm transport are higher and often include a demand charge that must be paid whether or not a certain volume of gas is used in a given month. Smaller customers generally receive firm service only. Terms of service include a priority system that determines which customers receive gas in times of shortages or physical problems on the LDC system. Transport customers are also subject to balancing charges. The LDC tariffs spell out the terms and conditions for how supply must match consumption and outlines the charges applied to customers who are out of balance.

Storage and Hub Services

As end users and marketers are now managing supply portfolios across LDC systems, there may also be a need for storage and hub services in the downstream sector. Services provided are similar to those provided in the midstream sector. Pricing for such services is often directly related to the balancing provisions of the LDC's tariffs since incurring balancing charges is an alternative to the use of storage and/or hub services.

Risk Management

Since end-use customers may now be subject to the price volatility associated with non-regulated commodity prices (or in some cases, regulated prices that change monthly based on market conditions), they may require price risk management products. These are often provided by gas marketing companies but may also be provided by merchant banks or other financial houses.

Behind-the-Meter Services

Behind-the-meter services are services that relate to natural gas usage, but that occur on the customers premises. Examples include appliance maintenance and repair, energy efficiency improvements, analysis and monitoring of energy usage, and financing of energy-using equipment.

End-use customers continue to have a need for more traditional energy services such as energy management. But in recent years, we have seen such energy services expand to include combined commodities (gas, electricity, propane, internet access, phone), facilities management, financing of energy-consuming assets, price risk management, and full energy outsourcing.

Contracts

As the natural gas marketplace continues to mature, gas transactions have become increasingly complex. The simple physical flow of one bundle of natural gas from wellhead to market may now result in a multitude of transactions. These include transportation agreements on gathering, interstate transmission, and local distribution pipelines; processing agreements; and numerous supply purchase agreements. In all likelihood each of these transactions is made according to a pre-arranged contractual arrangement.

A contract is a set of mutually enforceable promises. Contracts are critical since they define the exact relationship between two parties. Attorneys can argue long and hard over the exact definition of a contract, but a working definition might be "an agreement that includes a valid and legally acceptable offer and an acceptance of that offer, with a valid consideration, entered into by parties having the legal capacity to contract."

Given the volatility we have experienced in the energy markets over the last few years, the importance of solid contracts has become paramount. Too many market participants have been burned by their counterparties who either found they could make more money by delivering to another customer, or more often, have gone out of business before the service was fully delivered.

Supply Contracts

With the advent of deregulation, supply contracts were separated from transportation contracts. As we have seen, supply often changes hands a number of times between wellhead and burnertip, and each transaction in the chain requires a contract. Because of the multiple transactions involved, most end users simply contract for supply at the burnertip or with their LDC, and all upstream transactions are handled by intermediary parties such as marketers or producers.

KEY PROVISIONS OF A SUPPLY AGREEMENT

- Parties to agreement
- Term of agreement
- Delivery point
- Quantity
- Pricing provisions
- Take provisions
- Credit assurances
- Force Majeure
- Billing and payments
- Termination rights
- Dispute resolution

Supply contracts, once highly-regulated, may now be held by two unregulated parties. Critical terms include price, quantity, term, firmness of deliveries, penalties for over and under delivery, termination rights, and credit assurances by both parties. Pricing is increasingly tied to specific published standards including market price indexes, the utility's average cost of purchasing gas or to futures prices. Some supply contracts are structured so that the supplier takes the risk of price fluctuations in return for a premium over indexed prices. Other terms and conditions are highly negotiable and tailored to meet specific parties' needs.

Transportation Contracts

To move gas from the wellhead to market areas, it is often necessary to contract with numerous pipelines. These include gathering lines, interstate transmission lines, intrastate transmission lines, and LDCs. Because each pipeline has its own set of contracts, the process of securing transportation can often be complex.

Critical terms in a transportation agreement include regulatory authority, priority of service, term, quantity, gas quality, receipt and delivery points, rates, and termination rights. Often, the pipeline tariffs are incorporated by reference. Gathering lines may be regulated by either state commissions or by FERC, but in the United States they are increasingly unregulated. Transmission lines are regulated either by FERC or a state public utilities commission. Transportation contracts with regulated entities are usually standard form contracts approved in advance by the regulatory body. Regulatory approval is necessary since regulated utilities cannot provide services without authorization from the regulator. In addition to the transportation agreement, the full contract includes the terms and conditions laid out in the pipeline's tariffs. The terms and conditions of transportation arrangements can be critical in determining whether gas reaches markets at competitive prices.

KEY PROVISIONS OF A TRANSPORTATION AGREEMENT

- Parties to agreement
- Government authority
- Quantity
- Term of agreement
- Receipt and delivery points
- Operating procedures
- Rates
- Billing and payments
- Dispute resolution
- Reference to applicable tariffs
- Termination rights

What you will learn:

- Why the gas industry is regulated

- The historical basis for regulation

- Who regulates what

- How regulators establish rates and rules

- What tariffs are

- The rate case process

- What incentive regulation is and how it works

8

8

SECTION EIGHT: REGULATION IN THE GAS INDUSTRY

It is impossible to fully understand today's natural gas marketplace without a comprehensive understanding of the role of regulation. Regulation exists to ensure that customers of pipelines and public utilities are protected from a lack of competition. To protect the public interest, regulation defines the services that utilities and pipelines offer, sets rates to be charged for those services, prescribes accounting systems, enforces safety standards, and approves construction of major new projects.

As the energy marketplace changes, traditional concepts of regulation are also changing. Thus, an understanding of how regulation has evolved is critical to success in a gas marketplace that is both highly regulated and highly competitive. In this section we will explore who the state and national regulators are and how they determine the rules and rates for the services they regulate.

Why Regulate the Gas Industry?

The answer to this question is primarily due to the existence of monopolies in the industry. A monopoly is a business situation in which a corporation – through market power or a government-granted franchise – is either the only company conducting business in a given industry or the sole source of a specific commodity or service. A "natural monopoly" occurs in an industry where characteristics of the industry tend to result in monopolies evolving. An example is the gas utility industry where a proportionately large capital investment is required to produce a single unit of output and where large operations can provide goods or services at a lower average cost than can small operators. Both of these conditions occurred in the utility industry in the early 1900s. Thus, what began as a competitive utility market quickly evolved into a market with few competitors.

While this situation was ultimately deemed beneficial to the public, the extreme market power that resulted allowed utilities to provide services and set prices favoring certain customers and resulting in excessive profits. This then created the need for government oversight of these services.

The relationship between regulators and public utilities is often described as the "regulatory compact." This means that in return for government regulators granting exclusive service territories and setting rates in a manner that provides an opportunity for a reasonable return on investment, investor-owned public utilities submit their operations to full regulation. In the next section we will discuss how market forces evolving in the gas industry may require modification of the traditional regulatory compact for certain markets.

The Historical Basis for Regulation

In the mid to late 1800s, the utility industry rapidly developed in an environment of open competition. Most cities and states believed that competition between utilities kept prices down, and it was not uncommon to find cities with numerous utilities operating in open competition. In fact, competition became so fierce that price wars were common, often leading to the demise of all but one utility, which would then take advantage of the lack of competition by raising customers' rates exorbitantly! As the utility market evolved it became clear that its capital-intensive nature resulted in market inefficiencies (too much money spent on duplicative facilities) and allowed well-financed companies to push less successful ones out of the market.

To address this issue, state governments saw two options: municipal ownership of utilities or regulation of those that remained privately owned. In many states, it was the Railroad Commission (originally developed to oversee the expanding railroad industry) that was empowered to regulate the early gas and electric utilities. Established in 1885, the first energy-related regulatory agency was the Massachusetts Board of Gas Commissioners. Other states followed suit with the creation of their own public utilities commissions.

On the federal level, regulation was emerging as well. In 1887, the Interstate Commerce Act was enacted, which affected the transportation of goods and services across state lines – though an amendment to the act in 1906 specifically excluded the activities of natural gas pipelines. In 1938 the Federal Power Commission was created by the Natural Gas Act (NGA). This represented the first real regulation of the natural gas industry on a federal level. In a nutshell, the Natural Gas Act set reasonable rates for the sale of gas on interstate pipelines. These rates were calculated so that the pipelines could cover their costs of doing business and still make a fair rate of return. The NGA also set the requirements for the 7(c) certification process. This process, still in effect today, required pipelines to file for a Certificate of Public Convenience

8

and Necessity (CPCN) before building new facilities. Prior to granting such a certificate, the FPC would consider whether the facilities truly were in the best interest of the public. And finally, the NGA set out to ensure that pipelines did not discriminate in the provision of service to their customers and that rates could not be discounted without prior approval.

While comprehensive in its regulation, the NGA did not regulate the sale of gas at the wellhead from the producer to the interstate pipeline. In 1954, the Supreme Court changed this and empowered the FPC to regulate the price of gas sold into interstate commerce. Because oversight of individual producers was unworkable, the agency developed mandatory pricing based on a number of criteria. Unfortunately, the effect of this price fixing was to lower gas prices to such a degree that it was no longer profitable for producers to sell their gas into interstate commerce. Looking to increase profits, they began to focus on intrastate markets, which were not subject to the federal regulation. This resulted in highly limited availability of gas volumes in interstate markets.

In the 1970s, the OPEC oil embargo and other market forces caused severe shortages of natural gas. So severe that many people believed our supply would soon run out. The truth, however, was not that we were running out of the fuel – it was just not economical to produce at the below market rates set by the federal government. Attempting to allow a free market to resolve these shortages, the Natural Gas Policy Act of 1978 deregulated the price of gas at the wellhead and was the beginning of the deregulated market we know today. This deregulation caused a boom in the industry as producers saw rapidly rising prices and the opportunity for increased profits. With the opportunity for increased profits, drilling rates increased and new supply entered the market. Ultimately, this success led to deregulation across the gas industry sectors in the U.S. (and lower prices benefitting all consumers) as we will see in the next section on gas deregulation.

Who Regulates What?

Gas services on interstate pipelines (those that cross state lines) and storage services involved in interstate commerce are regulated by the Federal Energy Regulatory Commission (FERC). Gas services that are provided entirely within a given state by investor-owned utilities are regulated by the state's public utilities commission. Municipal utilities are generally regulated only by the local government authority (such as the city) although some states do regulate municipal utilities in some areas of their business. Some gas services such as certain commodity sales and over-the-counter financial products are only lightly regulated.

The Federal Power Commission and the Federal Energy Regulatory Commission

The regulatory agency created by the NGA was the Federal Power Commission. The original FPC was charged with a number of tasks:

- Regulate natural gas in interstate commerce.

- Promote the conservation of natural gas resources.

- Set out a uniform standard of accounting for interstate pipelines.

- Grant Certificates of Public Convenience and Necessity that would ensure that construction of pipeline facilities was always in the public interest.

- Require pipelines to provide service to local distribution companies.

- Authorize rates and tariffs and standardize contracts used for the sale and transportation of natural gas.

In 1974, the Department of Energy Organization Act created the Federal Energy Regulatory Commission (FERC), a successor agency to the FPC. For the natural gas industry (FERC also regulates electricity), FERC is now responsible for:

- Regulation of pipeline, storage and liquefied natural gas facility construction including issuing certificates for the construction of such facilities.

- Regulation of natural gas transportation in interstate commerce including determining services that pipelines offer and setting rates and terms of service for these services.

- Regulation of market behavior for entities trading gas in interstate commerce.

The FERC is led by five commissioners who are appointed by the President of the United States and confirmed by the Senate. Commissioners serve five-year staggered terms and each has an equal vote on all matters. The commissioners are supported by a staff of analysts and advisors.

State Regulation of the Gas Industry

The NGA did not authorize regulation of intrastate gas services (i.e. gas services provided only within state borders) by the federal government, so this regulatory responsibility fell on the states. State commissions are generally referred to as the Public Utilities Commission or Public Services Commission. The Hinshaw Amendment to the NGA allows states to regulate gas transportation and sale for resale of interstate gas as long as it is consumed within state borders (meaning that once gas enters the

8

state in which it will be consumed it is no longer subject to federal regulation as long as it stays within that state).

Perhaps the most important thing to note regarding state regulators is that no two agencies regulate exactly alike. Thus companies who do business in all 50 states essentially must deal with 50 different ways of doing business. State regulatory agencies are also responsible for gas deregulation in the states they regulate. So just as with state regulation, deregulation of the gas industry is inconsistent, with different rules and varying stages of deregulation in every state.

The Regulatory Process

An LDC or pipeline may provide services and charge rates only to the extent that those rates and services have been authorized by the appropriate regulatory commission. The commission authorizes services and rates by issuing decisions. Once a decision is issued, the various LDCs and pipelines develop tariffs (rules by which service is provided) that are in compliance with the terms and conditions set forth in the decision. Tariffs describe utility rates, rules, service territory, and terms of service. Before tariffs become effective, they must be approved by the regulators. And once approved and filed, it is unlawful for an LDC or pipeline to provide any service that deviates from what is described in its tariff.

Rates and rules are established through regulatory proceedings that are designed to give all interested parties a fair opportunity to state their opinions and present supporting facts. Regulatory proceedings include:

- Rulemakings — Proceedings held to establish new rules by which regulated entities conduct business.

- Rate cases — Proceedings that establish the rates an LDC or pipeline can charge for its services.

- Certificate cases — Proceedings that approve construction of new facilities.

- Complaint cases — Proceedings that evaluate complaints filed against utilities.

Following is a discussion of the general process used by regulators to set rates and rules for regulated services. Each regulator, however, may define this process in its own fashion.

The Initial Filing

A proceeding is typically initiated by a filing from a regulated entity (for rate cases and certificate cases) or by a market participant (for complaint cases). The documents filed are reviewed by the commission staff and a formal process is begun. Rulemakings are a bit different. They apply when a major restructuring or change in regulation is contemplated, and in this case the regulatory agency takes the lead. Thus they are initiated by the regulator, who prepares and publishes a proposed rulemaking that describes how the regulator suggests changing market rules and/or ratemaking.

Preliminary Procedures

Usually an Administrative Law Judge (ALJ) or one of the Commissioners is assigned responsibility for steering the case through the regulatory process. This person is charged with conducting the public hearings and with preparing a recommended decision for the full commission to consider. Prior to the start of the proceeding, a pre-hearing conference is often scheduled that allows any interested party to make an appearance and state the extent to which it will participate in the hearings. The party must identify the issues it will raise and is asked to state whether it will file briefs, submit evidence and/or cross-examine witnesses. These parties are then deemed intervenors in the case, and secure certain participatory rights in the proceeding. Following the pre-hearing conference, the ALJ or assigned Commissioner sets a date for hearings.

Hearings

Hearings are held to ensure the commission is aware of all important evidence relating to issues being considered. This is important because the commission must issue its decision solely based on the evidence presented in hearings (the evidentiary record). Prior to hearings, the intervenors generally file written documents (opening briefs) stating their position on the issues. Hearings are then held to provide evidence in support of the various parties' positions. Evidence may be entered through written documents (exhibits) or through written or oral testimony by witnesses. Witnesses are subject to cross-examination and all testimony is given under oath. Some bodies, such as FERC, depend mostly on paper hearings and rarely hold hearings with witnesses. In some cases, such hearings are replaced with technical conferences, where parties have an opportunity to state their positions but formal cross-examination is not used. At the conclusion of testimony, interested parties usually have another opportunity to file a written statement arguing their position (closing briefs), and then all parties have the opportunity to respond to each other's closing briefs (reply briefs). All closing and reply briefs are supposed to be based solely on the factual evidence presented in the hearings and no new evidence can be introduced at this point in the proceeding. Although this sounds like a very clearly defined process, it should be noted that commissions have wide latitude in how they run hearings and politics can often play a significant role in what occurs.

The Draft Decision

Following the hearings, a draft decision is issued by the ALJ or Commissioner, which is subsequently reviewed by the entire commission. Parties may file written comments on the draft decision for consideration by the full commission. Based on these comments, the ALJ or presiding Commissioner may revise his or her draft decision before submitting it to the full commission as the suggested action. The draft decision is by no means final, and represents only the opinion (educated, we hope) of the ALJ or assigned Commissioner. The commission as a whole decides on whether the draft decision or an alternative point of view will be final.

The Final Decision

After all comments have been filed, the full commission considers the draft decision at a hearing conference. Changes to the draft decision may be made by the Commissioners and occasionally two versions of a decision will be considered simultaneously. In this case, the decision different from the draft decision is called an "alternate decision." A decision becomes law when a majority of the Commissioners vote in support of it. At that point, it is called a final decision.

Review of Decisions

Any final decision is subject to review by the commission that issued it. Parties may request review either through a Petition for Modification or a Request for Rehearing. Petitions for Modification apply when a party believes that a decision fails to reflect the factual evidence presented in the evidentiary record. A Request for Rehearing applies when facts have changed since the evidentiary record was completed. If the commission denies review, or chooses to uphold the decision after review, the requesting party may ask the state (or U.S., depending on jurisdiction) courts to review the decision.

Tariffs

Tariffs are public documents, written by regulated entities and approved by the regulatory commission, that detail rates, rules, service territories, and terms of service. Tariffs are supposed to be written in accordance with the final decision of the regulatory body. Since decisions are often open to interpretation, tariffs must be approved by the regulatory body before they are legal. In general, tariffs include the following:

- A preliminary statement that describes the LDC's or pipeline's terms of service and service territory and sets forth the accounts and adjustment mechanisms used in revenue accounting.

- Rate schedules that define rates and other terms of service for specific classes of customers.

- Rules that detail terms and conditions for service not described in rate schedules.

- Sample forms, including all standard form contracts, approved contract deviations and other standard forms used in day-to-day business.

Tariffs that have been approved by a regulatory commission are binding legal documents which constitute the contract between the regulated entity and its customers. A regulated entity cannot change its tariffs or fail to follow any provision in its tariffs in any way without approval from the regulatory agency. Copies of entities' tariffs can usually be found on the company's website.

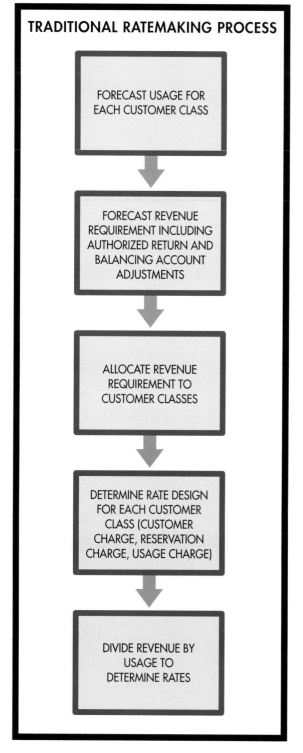

TRADITIONAL RATEMAKING PROCESS

FORECAST USAGE FOR EACH CUSTOMER CLASS

FORECAST REVENUE REQUIREMENT INCLUDING AUTHORIZED RETURN AND BALANCING ACCOUNT ADJUSTMENTS

ALLOCATE REVENUE REQUIREMENT TO CUSTOMER CLASSES

DETERMINE RATE DESIGN FOR EACH CUSTOMER CLASS (CUSTOMER CHARGE, RESERVATION CHARGE, USAGE CHARGE)

DIVIDE REVENUE BY USAGE TO DETERMINE RATES

Setting Rates through a Traditional Ratecase

A prime example of the regulatory process is ratemaking. One of the most important functions of the regulator is to set rates for monopoly services. The general concept of ratemaking is that monopoly entities are entitled to charge rates that will allow them to cover their costs of service, plus a reasonable rate of return (or profit) on capital invested by shareholders to build the necessary facilities to provide the service. The process of setting rates requires determining a revenue requirement that includes all the revenue the LDC or pipeline needs to collect to cover costs and make a reasonable return, and then translating that revenue requirement into specific rates for specific customers. This process is outlined below.

Forecasting Usage

So that variable expenses can be forecast and rates can be set such that they satisfy the revenue requirement, it is necessary to first forecast the number of customers and the overall demand and usage levels for each applicable customer class. This is generally done using historical data, demographic forecasts for regional growth, and estimates on how customers will use natural gas.

Determining a Revenue Requirement

A revenue requirement is defined as the total amount of money an LDC or pipeline must collect from customers to pay all operating and capital costs, including its return on investment. The revenue requirement is determined by forecasting expenses (operating and maintenance, administrative and generation, and taxes other than income taxes), depreciation, and income taxes for a rate cycle, and then adding to that the return on rate base plus any amounts (positive or negative) outstanding in the balancing account.

```
DETERMINING A
REVENUE REQUIREMENT

Expenses
+
Depreciation
+
Income Taxes
+
Rate Base x Authorized Rate of Return
+/−
Balancing Account Adjustment
```

The rate base is the depreciated value of all the capital facilities the LDC or pipeline has constructed in order to provide services to its customers. The return on rate base consists of two components – the return on debt and the return on equity. The return on debt is intended to reflect the cost of borrowing money to build facilities and is applied to the portion of the rate base that has been financed through borrowing. The return on equity is the amount of return that share-holders need to keep them from investing in some other business instead. This is applied to the equity portion of the rate base which is the portion built with shareholders' investment. The return on equity multiplied by the rate base multiplied by the percentage financed through shareholder investment is the primary component of profit for a monopoly LDC or pipeline.

A balancing account is an accounting mechanism that keeps track of the difference between the revenue requirement and the actual revenues obtained by the LDC or pipeline. Any differences covered by the balancing account are added to or subtracted from future revenue requirements, thus insulating the LDC or pipeline and its customers from risks of revenue deviations. Typical portions of the revenue requirement covered by balancing accounts for LDCs (but not usually pipelines) include expenses such as gas purchase costs and, in some states, revenue fluctuations due to increased or decreased weather-related usage. The use of balancing accounts to stabilize revenues associated with weather conditions is called weather normalization.

Revenue Allocation to Customer Classes

Once an overall revenue requirement for a service is established, it must then be determined what portion will be paid by each class of customer. This process is called revenue allocation. Various allocation methods are used in different situations. The most simple method (equal cents per therm) allocates costs based on usage. While simple, this approach is not necessarily an accurate way of assigning costs. Since many of the costs of a gas system are fixed, actual costs caused by customers are more likely to be based on the maximum demand that a customer puts on the system, and not on the amount of therms used. Thus a more common – though more complex – method is to allocate costs based on the estimated cost of service to each customer category (cost-of-service). This allocation can take into account demand-based costs as well as usage-based costs. An even more complex method (equal proportionate marginal costs or EPMC) allocates costs based on the marginal cost of serving each customer category. The marginal cost methodology looks at the cost of serving one additional increment in each class, rather than using the average cost as is done in the cost-of-service methodology. Actual determination of revenue allocation can be complex and is commonly one of the most highly contested issues in regulatory proceedings.

Determining Rate Design

Once a revenue requirement has been determined and allocated to the various customer classes, the rates that each customer class will pay are determined in the rate design phase of the proceeding. But before actual rates are set, the rate structure must first be determined. Rates are structured in any number of ways, but typically they are divided into three distinct components:

- Customer charges — A per-customer charge independent of usage.

- Reservation or demand charges — These charges are based on contract quantity or the maximum demand incurred within a specific timeframe, rather than actual variable usage.

- Usage or variable charges — These charges depend on actual usage. The usage charge is calculated by dividing the remaining required revenue (after accounting for customer and demand charges) by the forecasted usage for that class.

Much like revenue requirements were allocated to customer classes in a prior step, revenues within each customer class must be allocated to each charge type. Again, regulators generally attempt to do this based on the way that costs are actually incurred. For example, those costs associated with specific customer hookups are assigned to the customer charge, demand related costs are assigned to the demand charge, and variable costs are assigned to the usage charge.

Determining the Rate

Now that the revenue and the forecast usage associated with each charge type within each class have been determined, rates for each charge can be established by dividing the allocated revenue by the appropriate forecasted factor. For example, revenues allocated to usage charges for the residential class are divided by forecasted residential usage to create a rate in $/therms, while revenues allocated to the residential customer charge are divided by the forecasted number of customer accounts to create a customer charge in $/account.

Incentive Regulation

In recent years, regulators have begun to go beyond the traditional regulatory compact to create new ways of inciting efficient utility or pipeline performance. Incentive regulation generally avoids after-the-fact reasonableness reviews and offers the regulated entity the opportunity to profit from exceptional performance. Examples of incentive regulation include performance-based, benchmarking, rate caps, and market-based and are described in more detail below.

Performance-based

Performance-based regulation compares the LDC's performance to a market-index. An example might be procurement of gas supply for residential customers. The LDC's cost of buying gas would be compared with a market-index for gas prices in the LDC's area. If the LDC's cost is lower than the market-index, the LDC's shareholders and ratepayers split the savings. Conversely, if the LDC's cost of gas is higher, shareholders and ratepayers split the increased cost. This, of course, provides strong incentive for the LDC to pay close attention to its gas purchasing strategies.

Benchmarking

Benchmarking regulation sets rates in the first year of a rate cycle using traditional methods. For future years, rates are set by a formula that increases them based on an appropriate inflation index and then reduces them based on a regulatory-determined productivity factor that the utility is expected to achieve. This is often called x-y regulation where the factor x represents inflationary increases and factor y represents productivity-based decreases. This incites the utility to go out and find ways to enhance productivity and to keep costs below inflation since any difference between actual costs and revenues collected in rates is a cost/benefit to shareholders.

Rate Caps

Under rate cap methodology, fixed rates are set by the regulator for a period of years. Any variation between actual costs and revenues collected on the capped rates is a cost/benefit to shareholders.

Market-based

In rare cases where market forces are strong enough to prevent potential monopoly abuses, regulators have allowed LDCs and pipelines to charge market-based rates. In some cases the LDC's or pipeline's shareholders have been allowed to keep any benefits and in other cases benefits have been shared between ratepayers and shareholders. Market-based pricing runs counter to most regulators' philosophies and hence experiments in this area have been limited.

Service Standards

To ensure that LDCs or pipelines do not let service quality decline in the interest of achieving incentive revenue, regulators often create specific measurable service standards. Failure to achieve these standards results in shareholder penalties.

The Future of Regulation

As we will see in the next section, regulation of the gas industry has changed significantly over recent years. In the last few years, attention has been more strongly focused on changes in regulation of the electric industry. However, it is likely that we will see continued evolution in the way that regulation is applied to LDCs and gas pipelines.

What you will learn:

- How regulation has evolved over time

- What services have been deregulated on both state and federal levels

- How markets evolve over time in response to deregulation

- How deregulation efforts have fared to date

9

SECTION NINE: DEREGULATION

Recent Evolution of Gas Regulation

Both federal and state regulation of the gas industry have seen significant changes in recent years. The FERC and state regulatory agencies made significant changes to regulation in the 1980s, allowing numerous parties to hold pipeline capacity and transport their own gas supply, thus opening up today's competitive gas market. In several cases, they also reduced oversight on pipelines' decisions to construct new facilities by placing the return on such facilities fully at shareholder risk. Many state agencies have also begun to reduce regulatory oversight on utility gas purchasing for the core portfolio and other utility functions by approving incentive-based regulation. Further changes are likely to result in unbundling of transportation and distribution functions.

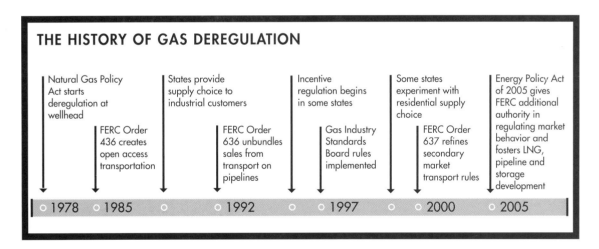

THE HISTORY OF GAS DEREGULATION

Natural Gas Policy Act starts deregulation at wellhead		States provide supply choice to industrial customers		Incentive regulation begins in some states		Some states experiment with residential supply choice		Energy Policy Act of 2005 gives FERC additional authority in regulating market behavior and fosters LNG, pipeline and storage development
	FERC Order 436 creates open access transportation		FERC Order 636 unbundles sales from transport on pipelines		Gas Industry Standards Board rules implemented		FERC Order 637 refines secondary market transport rules	
1978	1985		1992		1997		2000	2005

Federal Deregulation

The restructuring of the gas industry began in 1978 when Congress passed the Natural Gas Policy Act (NGPA), which deregulated the wellhead price of natural gas. Previously, wellhead prices had been controlled by a complex set of regulations that resulted in considerable restraint of supply. Deregulation of wellhead prices resulted in a temporary price increase, followed by increased development of reserves and ulti-mately more supply at lower prices. Today, most observers believe that over the long run market forces efficiently operate to keep supply and demand in check, and that consumers have benefitted from significant reductions in gas prices and ample supplies to meet market demand.

With prices deregulated, a spot market for natural gas arose. However, the ability of end-use markets to access spot gas was severely restricted because most interstate pipeline capacity was controlled by the pipelines themselves, which moved only the gas they owned. This "merchant gas" was purchased in supply basins under long-term contracts and resold to LDCs, also under long-term contracts. In the mid-1980s, the FERC acted to restructure the way interstate pipelines offered services. Through a series of orders, culminating in Order 636, the FERC restructured long-term commit-ments by pipelines and required all pipelines to become mere transporters of gas. Now, most pipelines offer limited supply services and act as "open access" or "common carri-ers" of other parties' gas supply. The major components of Order 636 include:

- Unbundled services — Pipelines are required to provide transportation services unbundled or separate from gas supply acquisition services.

- Capacity release — Pipelines are required to allow firm transportation customers to re-sell or broker their unused capacity to other users, thus creating a secondary transportation market.

- Straight Fixed Variable rate design — Pipeline rate structures were changed so that all fixed costs associated with transportation (including return on equity and associated taxes) are recovered through fixed reservation charges. This encourages holders of firm capacity to release their unused capacity to other parties since they pay full charges whether they use it or not.

Since the implementation of Order 636, the interstate transportation market has become increasingly competitive with capacity traded on a daily basis. Adept marketers have learned to use the secondary market to significantly reduce their costs of transportation.

State Deregulation

The initial impetus for state deregulation was the potential for bypass. Under federal regulation, large commercial and industrial customers are allowed to connect directly to an interstate pipeline, thereby bypassing LDC distribution service. Since bypass deprives the LDC of revenues that could support the LDC system for all customers, many states are happy to consider deregulating the market in order to keep these large customers on the LDC system. State deregulation of the gas industry continues on a state-by-state basis. In some states, LDC service has been unbundled so that third parties can sell supply directly to end-use customers, potentially reducing customer costs by fostering competition between sellers. Unfortunately, retail service to residential customers has yet to be fully successful. The map below shows the various stages of gas regulation currently found in each of the states and also highlights the inconsistency of deregulation across the U.S.

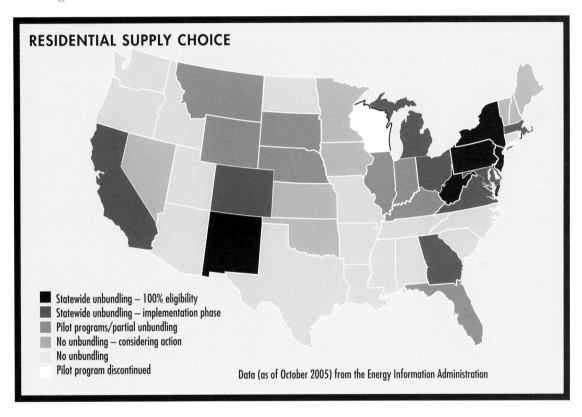

RESIDENTIAL SUPPLY CHOICE

- Statewide unbundling – 100% eligibility
- Statewide unbundling – implementation phase
- Pilot programs/partial unbundling
- No unbundling – considering action
- No unbundling
- Pilot program discontinued

Data (as of October 2005) from the Energy Information Administration

Today, nearly all large commercial and industrial end users may purchase supply from any party they choose and may also acquire interstate transportation in all 50 states. Thus the option is available to purchase supply at either the burnertip, in the supply basin itself or at a market center somewhere in-between. Because of the complexities of managing transportation, most end users purchase gas either at the burnertip or at the inlet to the LDC, using intermediary parties such as marketers to arrange transportation.

Many state regulatory commissions have also initiated reforms to replace regulatory oversight with performance risk for utilities. A good example is the core procurement function. Prior to performance-based ratemaking (PBR), utilities would purchase gas for their core customers as they saw fit, but were subject to reasonableness reviews at which their gas buying decisions were reviewed after the fact (a sort of regulatory Monday morning quarterbacking). If certain purchases were deemed "unreasonable," the utility stood to lose considerable money because the amount that was determined to be unreasonable had to be credited back to the ratepayers. This money is not recoverable from future rates, but rather paid by the shareholders. To make matters worse, there is no upside for the utility in a reasonableness proceeding.

Under PBR, the commission sets a benchmark it deems just and reasonable for the procurement of these supplies. The utility then sets out to beat the benchmark price. If it comes in just at the benchmark, it neither loses nor gains additional money. If it beats the benchmark, savings are usually shared between ratepayers and shareholders. And if it falls short, the additional costs are also shared between ratepayers and shareholders. PBR is often preferred by utilities because it sets standards and concrete targets before the gas purchases are made, not after. From the regulatory commission's perspective, this also avoids a costly reasonableness proceeding where the commission must study each expenditure to determine whether it was reasonable and should be included in rates. Such reforms increase the possible return that utilities can obtain, but also increase the risk that below standard returns will occur. More importantly, PBR gives the utility clear and consistent goals to meet in its performance – something certainly lacking in a reasonableness review. And it avoids what could be considerable costs to defend the utility's purchasing decisions. It is likely that PBR and other types of incentive regulation will continue to evolve as deregulation of the energy moves forward.

The Market Maturation Cycle

To truly understand the dynamics of the natural gas marketplace, it is important to understand the impacts of two conflicting forces – regulation and competition. Initially the gas industry evolved in a highly competitive environment. But as described earlier, the industry was soon viewed as a natural

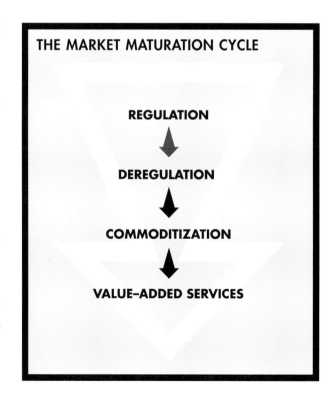

THE MARKET MATURATION CYCLE

REGULATION

↓

DEREGULATION

↓

COMMODITIZATION

↓

VALUE–ADDED SERVICES

GAS SERVICES IN THE MARKET MATURATION CYCLE

Regulation
• LDC services to residential and small commercial customers in most states

Deregulation
• LDC services to industrial customers
• LDC services to residential and small commercial customers in some states
• Interstate pipeline services

Commodity
• Gas sales to industrial customers
• Wholesale gas trading
• Upstream gas sales

Value-Added Services
• Behind-the-meter services to industrial and commercial customers
• Financial services

---

monopoly requiring considerable government oversight. Over time, virtually all of the industry became dominated by federal and state regulation. The last 30 years, however, have seen relaxation of regulation in many sectors of the industry, leading to the return of more market-based dynamics. This process is called the market maturation cycle.

The four stages of the market maturation cycle – regulation, deregulation, commoditization, and value-added services – provide an excellent framework from which to review the evolution of the natural gas industry. While many segments of the industry will likely mature through these stages, they may not do so simultaneously. For instance, local distribution is still regulated as a monopoly function while interstate pipelines are generally deregulated. Gas supply – and even gas transportation in many places – are traded as a commodity while gas marketers offer value-added services in an attempt to distinguish their products from the competition.

Regulation

This phase is characterized by increasing regulation as a means of managing rapid growth and ensuring that consumers are protected from monopolistic practices. Transactions are highly structured and usually long-term in nature. Prices are fixed, buyers and sellers are relatively few, and barriers to market entry are significant. Transactions generally occur between large entities and are subject to standard regulatory rules. Prices are cost-based, with little or no flexibility.

Prior to the implementation of the Natural Gas Policy Act in 1978, the entire natural gas industry was in the regulation phase of the market maturation cycle. Gas prices were regulated at the wellhead. Once the gas made its way to an interstate pipeline, transmission charges were regulated as well, with pipeline service available to only a few buyers. At the LDC citygate, the gas was sold to the LDC and distributed to end users at rates that were set according to customer class. As you have seen, the industry gained little from competition and customers had virtually no choice in the services offered to them.

Deregulation

In this phase, rules are loosened and barriers to entry are broken down. As the number of competitors increases, transactions become more flexible and customers attempt to benefit from increasing choice and competition. Regulation still controls much of the way business is transacted and is designed to encourage a level playing field among competitors. In the deregulation phase of the cycle transactions become specialized and are tailored to the individual customer. Pipeline and LDC prices are still basically cost-based but flexibility in pricing to meet competition is often allowed. Performance-based ratemaking (setting performance targets upon which rates are based) is often adopted, allowing the pipeline or LDC to make or lose money depending on its performance relative to predetermined targets.

Wellhead pricing was the first area of the gas industry to experience deregulation, followed by interstate pipelines. As this occurred, pipelines were allowed some leeway in the rates they charged and anyone who was deemed creditworthy could buy space on the pipe. Eventually, a secondary market evolved where holders of pipeline capacity could buy and sell space at prices that began to reflect actual market conditions. Deregulation has also occurred on the LDCs for most large commercial and industrial end users who can now buy their gas supply from the marketer of their choice.

Commoditization

In this phase of the market maturation cycle, prices are market-sensitive and highly volatile. Regulations act mainly to prevent price manipulation. Transactions become simplified and transferable among buyers and sellers and a futures market develops where obligations to buy or sell are freely traded. Transactions that used to be secured with a handshake between old friends are now handled electronically with buyers and sellers often blind to each other's identity. Pipeline and LDC prices become market-based where sufficient competition exists for their services and regulation is no longer a controlling factor.

Gas supply is a perfect example of the commoditization stage. In today's industry, gas can be bought in any number of ways: futures, long-term contracts, on the spot market, or even on an hourly basis. And prices are now reflective of market conditions with pricing based purely on supply and demand. As is typical of this phase, the commodity marketplace has many buyers and sellers, there is price transparency, no one entity has market power, and there are no barriers to transfer of the commodity.

Value-Added Services

In this final phase of the market maturation cycle, participants attempt to add value (and increase profit) by adding services their customers will value to the sale of commodity. In many instances, deregulation has led to razor thin commodity margins, so marketers are forced to develop customer-focused services that will improve profits to the seller. Because one molecule of methane gas is pretty much the same as another, value-added services are the best way for participants to increase market share.

In today's gas marketplace, most retail gas marketers rely on value-added services to increase both market share and profits. Services offered include facilities management (in which they will monitor and maintain a customer's equipment), energy management (in which they will study the customer's usage patterns and offer suggestions on how to decrease energy costs), and pricing and risk management services (in which energy pricing matches the customer's risk profile). In addition, as marketers attempt to access residential and small commercial customers, they may offer services such as combined commodity (where gas service is combined with other utility services such as electricity, water, broadband, and cable) in an attempt to woo customers away from their local utility service.

We've now seen how the natural gas industry has matured through the market maturation cycle. It is important to remember that various areas of the industry mature at different times. Thus, even now we still have pieces of the industry in all four stages of the cycle. With this in mind, let's take a look at the effect this process has had on the various market participants who provide services to the industry.

The Regulated and Competitive Delivery Chain

As we've seen, prior to the beginnings of gas deregulation the natural gas delivery chain was quite simple: natural gas producers explored for and produced natural gas in the supply basins, sold it to interstate pipeline companies who delivered it to the city-gate where it was sold to the local distribution company for ultimate delivery to end users. For much of the delivery chain prices were regulated, so end users had little control over their energy costs. The only choice, really, was how much gas to use.

In the 25 or so years since the Natural Gas Policy Act of 1978, the natural gas marketplace has been predominantly deregulated. With this deregulation, the industry has seen two major shifts: many more participants have entered the marketplace, and because of this influx of competition, many large end users now have a myriad of choices. You can see clearly from the figure below the increased complexity that has resulted from opening up the gas marketplace to competition. Not only are there more

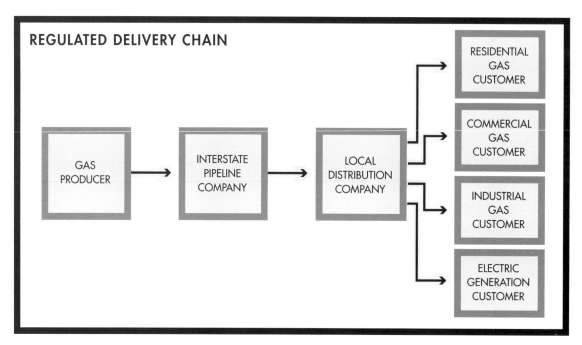

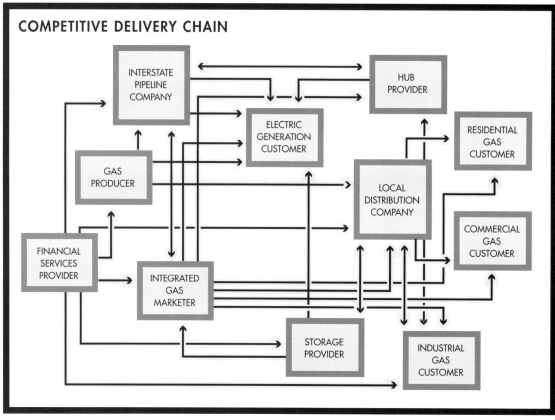

9

ATLANTA GAS LIGHT

In April 1997, the Georgia General Assembly passed legislation offering Georgia gas utilities the option to unbundle distribution services for core customers. Atlanta Gas Light (AGL), the major LDC in Georgia, opted to shift its role from the sale and distribution of natural gas (bundled service) to just its distribution. As the first such program to attempt this in the United States, the Georgia experiment has been closely watched. Here's how the plan was structured.

Beginning in the fall of 1998 all gas customers in AGL's service were required to begin choosing a third-party natural gas marketer from whom they would purchase natural gas supply. Once 33% had done so, the remaining customers were required to switch within 100 days or be randomly assigned to one of the approved marketing companies. Throughout this process, customer choice was promoted as you might expect – lower prices, better customer service, bundled service, more options, etc. Marketers were required to be certified by the Georgia Public Service Commission (PSC), which assured customers that each company would meet stringent requirements designed to protect them.

Several years later, the results are mixed. Price levels in Georgia are generally similar to surrounding states. In the initial years of deregulation, service problems and price volatility (due to cold weather, not deregulation) eroded public perceptions. At one time 24 companies were on the PSC's list of approved marketers. After several declared bankruptcy and others exited due to disillusionment with the market, 11 companies were active in 2005. Review by the State of Georgia resulted in some market modifications such as introducing a state-regulated service provider option, but concluded that it did not make sense for the state to roll-back deregulation. In recent years the market has stabilized and customers have become accustomed to supply choice. Some beneficial new pricing options such as fixed rates have emerged, but the jury is still out as to whether major benefits have materialized.

One lesson the AGL experience has made clear is that implementing full deregulation is a lengthy process and benefits may not be realized overnight. It is important to remember that Georgia was the first state to attempt such a comprehensive deregulation effort. When moving forward with new ideas, regulators, utilities, marketers, and customers must plan for the stamina required to work through the inevitable stumbling blocks.

players in the competitive delivery chain, but interaction between them is no longer linear as it was when the industry was highly regulated.

The million dollar question, of course, is does this new market structure work more efficiently than the regulated and vertically-integrated delivery chain we knew 25 years ago? The answer probably depends upon whom you ask! For some, the confusion and hassle of choosing a service provider is not worth the small savings they've enjoyed on their gas bills. Consider the deregulation of the telephone industry. While we've all come to rely on services such as call waiting, call forwarding, caller ID, etc., does anyone really enjoy the relentless telemarketing Sprint and Verizon employ to sell them?

For others – large industrial gas users for example – the competitive delivery chain has offered tremendous opportunities. Lower prices, creative service options and the ability to choose an energy provider have been well worth the effort to open up the natural gas marketplace.

9

What you will learn:

- How supply and demand fluctuate

- Factors impacting market-based pricing

- Why gas prices are so volatile

- The status of the wholesale market

- The status of the retail market

SECTION TEN: MARKET DYNAMICS

Ultimately, all economics of the marketplace are dictated by the end user, who will purchase gas only so long as it is financially feasible to do so. (Even a residential customer will eventually stop his usage of gas if prices become too high.) If an alternate fuel is available at a lower cost, the end user will not buy gas, but rather meet his energy needs with the alternate fuel. And when gas is the most economic fuel, end users who have a choice of supplier are likely to switch gas suppliers very quickly if one offers a better price than another (this is called "gas-on-gas competition"). Again, gas is a commodity, and the source and supplier of a commodity is mostly irrelevant.

The gas marketplace in the U.S. and Canada has become a "continental market" where pipelines are interconnected and access between multiple supply basins and market regions is widespread. Therefore, the dynamics of this market are fairly straightforward: purchasers of gas chase the cheapest supply and sellers of gas chase market areas offering the highest profits. Since supply basins are closely linked, prices in all regions adjust quickly to account for changes in other areas. Such price correlation is possible due to an integrated pipeline market, price discovery, open electronic trading, and the robust natural gas futures market.

Supply and Demand

For years, the gas industry has been characterized by boom and bust cycles. As we move into a competitive marketplace, we continue to see market perceptions of supply and demand fluctuating rapidly from severe shortage to severe oversupply in a period of just a few months. Typically, the perception of low supply leads to significant increases in prices – which in turn leads to perceived profit opportunities and willingness among financiers to provide capital for drilling and pipeline expansion. At the same time, demand is reduced in reaction to the high prices. The resulting increase in supply and reduction in demand rapidly drives prices back down. All the market participants who once had dollar signs in their eyes now groan in frustration and regret all the money they spent. As the old gas patch statement goes: "Please God, give me one more boom, this time I promise not to waste it away!"

Historically, demand in the gas industry was driven primarily by weather and the general industrial business cycle. More recently we have seen the increasing influence of electric demand as gas-fired generation has become the largest new source of electricity.

As this book goes to print in late 2005, concerns over gas supply again dominate the marketplace. Despite historically high prices and high drilling rates, new production has failed to keep up with growth in natural gas demand. Heightened by hurricane damage to gas production facilities in the Gulf of Mexico, the concern over supply availability has driven natural gas prices to all time highs in the fall of 2005. It remains to be seen whether the historical pattern of high prices followed by a flood of new supplies entering the market will again occur.

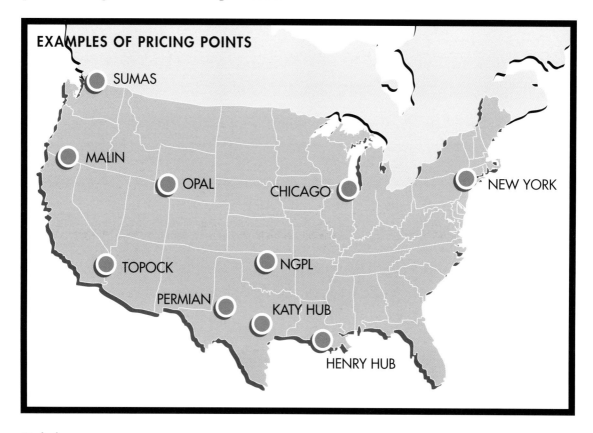

EXAMPLES OF PRICING POINTS

Pricing

Various factors influence the price of natural gas at any given location. From a very basic standpoint, the price is determined by supply and demand (including perceptions of the future balance of supply and demand). Key factors include the number of buyers and sellers in the market, projections for future supply and demand, weather, the amount of gas in storage, the projected cost of future supply (or the replacement cost), market alternatives for suppliers, supply alternatives for buyers, transport constraints, and general market psychology.

Indexes

A basic requirement for a commodity market is open price discovery. This means that all participants have access to information about the market price of gas at specific locations. Indexes, compiled by buyers and sellers reporting trades and prices to an impartial third party, provide this information. Unfortunately, indexes can be misleading because they depend on accurate reporting from buyers and sellers and also require a large number of transactions to be statistically valid, neither of which can always be counted on. Given recent revelations about false price reporting in the gas industry, FERC and various market participants are working together to develop improved ways to determine valid public indexes.

Price Volatility

Price volatility, or the movement of price over time, was once measured over a period of years. In today's fast-paced market, price volatility is often experienced on a daily basis. Up until the emergence of an electricity commodity marketplace, natural gas had been the most volatile commodity ever traded. In fact, monthly price fluctuations of up to 100% have not been unusual in recent years!

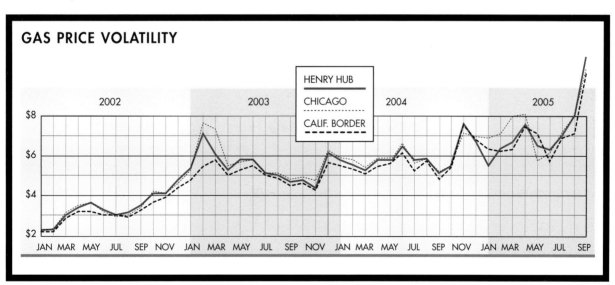

This extreme volatility has resulted in the need for sophisticated risk management techniques, which we will discuss later in this book.

Netback and Netforward Calculations

Producers measure the value of any given sale on the basis of a netback calculation. This calculation takes the price of gas in the marketplace and subtracts the transportation cost plus gathering and processing costs, if applicable, thereby netting a price in the supply basin. Producers with market alternatives will calculate the netback from various markets to determine market is most lucrative.

Buyers of gas often make the same sort of calculation, but beginning with the cost of supply in the basin and adding the various transportation and processing costs. This is called a netforward calculation.

The Wholesale Market

The wholesale market refers to gas transactions that occur between two parties, neither of which is the ultimate consumer of the gas. In the United States and Canada, a robust wholesale marketplace has evolved over the last ten years. Characteristics of this market include many buyers and sellers (a so-called "liquid market"), prices determined by market conditions, price transparency, no individual or group of companies with market power, and no barriers to transfer of goods (an integrated pipeline network without major constraints). Although some of the market perturbations of 2001 and 2002 (see box) caused concerns, the subsequent recovery of the marketplace appears to demonstrate that these healthy conditions exist throughout most of the U.S. and Canada.

A COMPETITIVE MARKET?

In 2001-2002 the gas markets were hit with a number or perturbations that raised questions about whether North America had as robust and competitive a gas market as many believed. Events that occurred include:

- The bankruptcy of Enron, the largest trader of natural gas in North America.

- Revelations that numerous companies had engaged in questionable accounting and other business practices.

- Exposure of widespread abuse of round-trip trading (round-trip trades are duplicative trades made by two parties that cancel each other out, but allow the parties to report increased transaction volumes, and perhaps to manipulate reported trade price data).

- False reporting by trading companies to publications that calculate market indexes.

- A finding by FERC that El Paso Pipeline Company manipulated markets by refusing to transport as much gas as its pipeline was capable of carrying.

These events led to a general questioning and mistrust of those engaged in gas trading and marketing, and contributed to the eventual crash in many of their stock market values. A number of companies who had been the largest natural gas traders were forced to leave the trading business and to sell off assets such as pipelines and natural gas reserves. By 2004 a market renewal was underway and by 2005 a new generation of market leaders had emerged.

As gas deregulation occurred at the wellhead in the late 1970s, an important role evolved for gas marketers – matching supply with end-use or downstream purchasers' demand. A gas marketer is an entity that creates value by connecting producers with consumers and by managing transportation, storage and risk to reduce the overall price of gas while ensuring that it is available when needed. By the late 1990s, the large integrated marketing firms dominated the gas marketplace with increasingly sophisticated trading and risk management strategies. During this time, it was not uncommon for natural gas to change hands numerous times between wellhead and the citygate.

Strategies practiced by the marketing companies included:

TRADING STRATEGIES		
Pure Trading	Structured Trading	Asset-based Trading
Buy low, sell high	Buy low, sell high, and take on added risks for a premium	Find most optimal way to sell long-term assets that you control

Unfortunately, the unbridled desire for growth coupled with some less than admirable business behaviors and difficult business conditions led to a crash in the fortunes of numerous large energy marketing companies in 2001 and 2002 (the spectacular failure of Enron being the most visible). By 2005 the wholesale market appears to have recovered and hopefully stronger market players have emerged. After all, trading must go on. Producers must find customers and LDCs and end users must find supply. Many larger producers have renewed their trading functions while new regional marketers and merchant banks have expanded their market presence to fill the void left by the market shakeout.

The Retail Market

Unlike the wholesale market which is extremely sensitive to price considerations, the retail market is much more service and relationship based. Most end-use customers see gas as a fundamental necessity for their homes and businesses, but cannot afford to focus too much on the day-to-day transactions. For this reason, they are more likely to pay a premium to receive good service. A recent McKinsey company survey in the European marketplace, which has seen a high level of retail competition, found that a majority of customers were turning away from the lowest-cost options, feeling they had been burned by the sub-standard service provided by low-cost providers. The majority of customers were more attracted to low-hassle and technology-based services.

In the United States and Canada, large consumers of natural gas have become accustomed to high quality retail services. These are generally provided by the marketing business units of large producers and integrated energy companies. These companies provide full supply services (meaning that the marketing company takes care of all transportation and supply arrangements) and often include numerous other behind-the-meter options in their menu of services.

In states where supply choice is available to smaller customers, the diversity of services available is much more limited. Most producers and integrated energy companies have found that potential profits do not reflect the risks associated with providing retail services to the masses. Barriers to success include customer access rules that vary from state-to-state, lack of access to smaller customers in some areas, the need for an expensive and sophisticated billing, credit and collections system, and a general lack of interest among consumers. But this is not to say that residential and small commercial customers will never benefit from retail competition. A few companies are beginning to create success in regional or other carefully chosen markets. Over time, the U.S. and Canada markets may follow European markets where retail customer choice has become an accepted way of doing business and where retail marketing companies compete vigorously for market share.

10

What you will learn:

- How various market participants create profits

- How profits are created under traditional and incentive ratemaking

- Key skills for creating profits

- What risk management is and why it's important

- How market participants manage risk using physical and financial instruments

- The difference between hedging and speculating

- What futures and options are and how they're used

- How Value at Risk (VAR) is used to measure risk levels

11

SECTION ELEVEN: MAKING MONEY & MANAGING RISK

Of course, the ultimate goal for all market participants is to make money. But since large portions of the industry continue to be dominated by regulated monopolies, the basic concepts that apply to making money (i.e., ensuring that revenues exceed costs) do not necessarily apply to all the entities we have studied. Nor is there always a strong incentive to develop products and services solely focused on customer desires (since much of the ability to make money for a regulated entity is determined by regulators, not customers). The gas industry is further complicated by the unique mixture of regulated and non-regulated entities, as well as the variation of regulation from state-to-state and from pipeline-to-pipeline. Thus it is critically important to understand the differing profit motivations of various market participants and how each makes money.

KEY SKILLS FOR PROFITABLE BUSINESSES		
Non-Regulated	Traditional Regulation	Incentive Regulation
• Marketing/pricing • Asset management • Financial management • Customer service • Billing • Credit and collections • Efficient operations • Information technology	• Regulatory/government relations • Expense containment • Asset expansion • Service reliability	• Purchasing • Expense containment • Productivity enhancement • Marketing/pricing • Information technology • Achieving service standards

As we study the various ways in which market participants make money, we must also consider the inherent risks involved at all levels of the business. When we talk about risk, we mean the possibility that earnings will be lower than projected, or lower than the market will support at the time products or services are delivered. Thirty years ago, a section on risk in a book on the natural gas industry would have been very short. With all aspects of the industry regulated, the biggest risk a pipeline or LDC faced was regulatory – the risk that regulators would lower its rate of return or otherwise rule against it. Today we can't open a newspaper without seeing the extent to which industry players are continually at risk. In this section we'll also take a look at the various risks faced by gas market participants and the tools they employ to mitigate them.

How Market Participants Create Profits

A company's profits are simply the difference between revenues and expenses. Revenues are determined by the amount of products or services sold multiplied by the price that is charged. In a non-regulated environment, businesses attempt to set their prices so that earnings are maximized. This is determined by an analysis of the business' competition and the profits that can be attained at various pricing levels. The optimal price, however, is determined by market forces. Historically, utilities' prices – or rates – have been determined based on the cost of providing service and not on market conditions.

Under traditional cost-of-service regulation, a revenue requirement is determined so that all of a utility's costs – including a return on investment (profit) – are covered. Balancing accounts are used to ensure that utilities collect no more and no less than the approved revenues. The utility's earnings result from the return portion of the revenue requirement. In recent years, regulators have begun to experiment with incentive ratemaking. Clearly, the different ways of making money make for very different business models and corporate motivations.

WAYS TO MAKE PROFITS		
Non-Regulated	Traditional Regulation	Incentive Regulation
• Revenues exceed costs • Physical marketplace • Financial marketplace	• Increase authorized rate base • Reduce expenses • Increase authorized return	• Increase revenues • Reduce expenses/capital • Produce/buy below baseline • Achieve service standards

How a Utility/Pipeline Makes Money – Traditional Method

Using traditional methodology, earnings are generally determined by the rate of return on equity authorized by the commission multiplied by the cost of facilities in the rate base. Because earnings are dependent upon the value of the rate base, utilities have traditionally been incited to invest in more facilities, thereby increasing their potential earnings. To protect the customer from paying for unnecessary facilities, regulators require prior approval of major facility additions (called Certificates of Public Convenience and Necessity) as well as reasonableness reviews of expenditures.

Under traditional regulation, a utility can increase earnings in three ways: increase rate base, increase the commission-approved rate of return on rate base, and in some cases, hold expenses below the forecast used to set rates. The latter strategy works if expenses or a portion of them are not subject to balancing account protection. So if an LDC is able to get regulators to approve a certain expense threshold, and then subsequently beats that threshold, it gets to keep as profit any remaining expense dollars. Various regulatory authorities have different ways of treating expenses, so sometimes this option is available to LDCs and pipelines and sometimes it is not.

It is important to keep in mind that rates of return are not guaranteed by regulators. LDCs or pipelines can fall short of authorized returns in many ways. One area of risk is called "disallowances." If regulators believe that utilities have failed to act prudently in spending money, the money spent can be disallowed, meaning that the utility is not allowed to include the expenditures in its revenue requirement. A second area of risk is expenses that are not balancing account protected. In this case, exceeding forecasted expenses would result in lower returns. Lastly, some LDCs do not have balancing account protection for revenue fluctuations due to weather. This means that should the LDC experience a warmer than usual winter, resulting in lower gas usage, revenues will be reduced. If there is no balancing account protection (so-called "weather normalization") then the utility will fall short of earnings projections. (Conversely, if it is colder than projected earnings may increase.)

How a Utility/Pipeline Makes Money – Non-traditional Methods

As the gas business becomes further deregulated and regulatory proceedings become more and more adversarial, regulators are struggling with ways to reform the regulatory process. Some traditional cost-of-service regulation is being replaced with incentive or performance-based regulation, which creates shareholder incentives for utilities to lower costs and reduce rates. Because reasonableness reviews are lengthy, and put a great strain on a utility's financial and human resources, many utilities would prefer to accept the risks and rewards of incentive regulation. Under incentive regulation, pipelines and utilities can increase profits by achieving or exceeding standards or goals set by the regulator. For more information on incentive regulation, please see the discussion on page 81.

How Unregulated Market Participants Make Money

Unlike regulated entities, other market participants' profitability is driven by the harsh realities of market dynamics. These include whether the participant is selling a service that the market is willing to buy, whether the participant is able to provide that service at a cost that still provides a reasonable profit given the price the market is willing to pay, and whether the participant is able to deliver the service after the product has been sold. In a volatile, fast-moving marketplace, many entities have discovered that bankruptcy is only a heartbeat away! As the gas business matures, strategies for profitability have begun to resemble strategies used by other competitive companies such as airlines and consumer product manufacturers.

Risk Management

Recent events in the gas business make it very clear that no matter how a market participant makes money, the levels of risk encountered in the marketplace are so extreme that companies can go from apparent profitability to insolvency in the course of a few short months. All market participants must actively and thoroughly manage their risks at all times. If they aren't doing this, they are placing their shareholders' investment in severe jeopardy.

As we have seen, natural gas prices have proven to be highly volatile. The graph below shows prices for three different pricing points (Henry Hub, Chicago and the California border) over several years. As you can see, prices varied dramatically. For example, prices at Chicago ranged from a low of $2.23 in January of 2002 to a high of $11.17 in

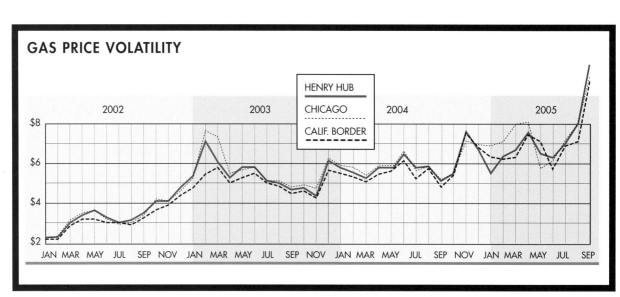

GAS PRICE VOLATILITY

September of 2005. (That's more than five times the January 2002 price, and potentially a huge loss to an unsuspecting marketer or end user who is at risk for such price fluctuations.)

Gas prices vary geographically as well. In the graph on page 108 you can see that while prices generally track from one pricing point to the other, there are at times substantial differences. Considering the small margins to be gained on commodity sales, this risk is substantial.

Major risks in the gas business include:

- Adverse price movements — The risk that prices will move in the opposite direction to what the participant desires.

- Volume risk — A customer does not use as much gas as the supplier anticipated, or a customer uses more gas than was contracted for.

- Basis risk — Prices at the point of purchase moved differently from the index used to hedge risk, or differently from prices at the location used to set the contract price.

- Counterparty risk — The risk that any party you do business with will not honor its commitments.

- Execution risk — You somehow fail to execute a transaction properly (e.g., a contract is not signed or a contractual condition not met).

- Tariff or regulatory risk — The regulator changes the rules for a business transaction after you have signed a contract.

- Operational risk — An asset you counted on fails to operate as expected.

Choices for Managing Risks

Means for managing risks include developing and implementing a thorough internal risk management policy, measuring risk levels on a daily or hourly basis, structuring of physical transactions, use of financial instruments, and careful management of counterparty relationships. Following are descriptions of the most common risk management techniques used in the gas industry today.

Physical Risk Management

Risk can be managed by simply structuring physical deals in a way that limits potential risk. This can include fixed pricing, pricing tied to market indexes and limits on volumes of gas a marketer is willing to provide at a particular cost. Other means of physical risk management include setting up alternative contracts with other suppliers, building a portfolio of deals so you aren't too exposed to any single deal and taking ownership of assets.

Any marketer would prefer to make only transactions that are structured in such a way that margins are locked in before the transaction is committed. The problem is that such a requirement can severely limit the number of transactions available. Another problem with physical deals is that they can be difficult to unwind (or get out of) if the market changes. Thus, market participants often depend on a combination of physical deal structure and more liquid financial instruments to manage risk exposures.

Financial Risk Management

The use of financial instruments to manage risks has been well known in commodity industries for decades. As the natural gas industry became deregulated, the principles used in other industries were applied to the gas business and the availability of financial instruments is now quite robust. Instruments used to shift risk include futures, options and over-the-counter (OTC) derivatives. Used properly, financial instruments match up parties wanting to speculate with those wanting to hedge (reduce risk), or in some cases, can allow both parties to a transaction to reduce their risk exposures or increase their profit potential.

For example, a producer needs to borrow money to cover the up-front costs of drilling a well and plans to pay back her loan by selling the gas over time as it is produced. However, since the producer is unsure what the value of the gas will be when she produces it, she cannot guarantee that she can make the loan payments. If the producer does not have other assets to ensure her ability to pay back the loan, she may need to use a financial instrument to lock in a guaranteed price for the gas up-front (and in turn qualify for financing of her operation).

Similarly, an end user that uses substantial amounts of gas does not know how much to budget if gas prices are uncertain. Prices higher than expected could result in negative cash flow and poor production decisions. Prices lower than expected might be a small windfall, but most end users prefer not to take such risks. The financial market offers opportunities to lock in prices for a year at a time.

And finally, marketers make money on small margins gained from buying and selling gas. If the value of the gas changes between buying and selling, the marketer can end up with a negative margin on a deal. So marketers may also use financial instruments to lock-in margins before entering into a deal. (See example of hedging on page 111.)

A SIMPLE EXAMPLE OF HEDGING

You are a marketer who buys gas each month to supply your markets. It is early March and you want to lock in a deal for April with an LDC that wants Permian supply at a fixed price. You might structure the transaction and cover your risk as follows:

- You and the end user agree on a fixed price of $9.65 for supply to be delivered in April.

- As the marketer, you have agreed to sell physical gas that you don't have yet, so you are at extreme price risk since you might end up buying gas at a higher price than you sell it for (a good way to lose money and go out of business fast!).

- To cover your price risk, you buy NYMEX April futures to match the volume of the physical deal. Since your point of sale is the Permian Basin, you still have the basis risk between the Permian Basin and Henry Hub, but history shows these prices generally move together. NYMEX April futures are selling for $9.67.

- When bidweek arrives, you go into the market to buy gas for delivery to the LDC. You discover that you underestimated the price when you sold to the LDC, and the gas price is actually $9.71. You also check your screen and see that NYMEX futures for April have gone up to $9.74. You buy the gas and sell the futures.

- If you had not bought futures, you would have bought gas at $9.71 and sold it at $9.65, for a loss of $0.06/MMBtu. But with hedging, you sell your futures at a profit, thus covering your physical loss:

Date	Cash Deal	Futures Deal
March 7	$9.65 sold	$9.67 bought
March 26	$9.71 bought	$9.74 sold
Net	($0.06) loss	$0.07 gain

Net gain on sale is $0.01/MMBtu. If you hadn't made the financial deal to hedge, you would have lost $0.06/MMBtu. (The LDC, by the way, is extremely pleased with your performance because it sees its supply cost $0.06/MMBtu less than the market price!)

Speculation versus Hedging

To understand the use of financial instruments, you must clearly understand the difference between hedging and speculation. Hedgers reduce risk by paying a third party to assume that risk, much like a homeowner pays an insurance company to assume the risk of rebuilding his house in the event of a fire. Speculators, on the other hand, take on risk in the hopes of making money (for instance, if the insurance company takes in more money than it pays out in all of its fire claims, it has speculated successfully on the risk of its customers' fire losses).

On the other side of each transaction is a financial services company hoping to profit by taking on the risk of price volatility. This is achieved by charging a fee for the service, or more commonly, by adding a margin into any price guarantee. For instance, if you were going to offer a product guaranteeing price, you might project the expected price level, add a few cents to cover the risk and add a couple more cents for profit. It is critical for both sides of a transaction to carefully track what risk has been assigned to what party, and who is hedging versus speculating. Most of the negative stories about use of financial derivatives have occurred because firms were speculating and misjudged the level of risk, or because firms thought they were hedging but did not properly understand the level of risk to which they remained exposed.

Hedging Techniques

Prices can be hedged in a variety of ways. Four common techniques are used in the gas business:

- Buying or selling at a fixed price — This requires no financial instruments and is simply handled through pricing of the physical gas sale. For instance, a marketer may agree to sell natural gas to a Texas end user for one year at a price of $5.50/MMBtu. Because the price is fixed, the end user has no price risk for that year. While the marketer has no price risk on the sale side of the transaction, she may be open to extreme risk if she hasn't locked in adequate gas supply at a specific price to cover the deal.

- Buying or selling futures — A future is an agreement to buy or sell a specific amount of gas at a specific location at a specified date and price. All futures are traded through a central exchange (NYMEX) that also guarantees performance of counterparties. Gas prices at specific locations can be locked in by buying or selling natural gas futures. Currently, the only natural gas futures in the U.S. are offered by NYMEX at Henry Hub in Louisiana. Because of our integrated pipeline network, futures at Henry Hub are commonly used to hedge risk across the U.S. and Canada. Most futures positions are not closed out by actual delivery but simply through buying or selling at a later date through the exchange. Many parties like to use futures since the exchange guarantees performance and transaction costs are low. However, if you are using the futures position to guarantee price at a location other than the actual delivery location, you are taking the risk that prices at your location will not track the futures price (basis risk).

- Buying or selling options — An option is a right, but not an obligation, to purchase or sell a future at a specific price within a specific time frame. Options are used to create price ceilings and floors rather than an absolute price guarantee. Options are also offered through the NYMEX at Henry Hub. There are two types of options. A call option grants the buyer the right to purchase a future at a specific price while a put option grants the right to sell a future at a specific price. The cost of this right is called the option premium. For the buyer, the risk of the option is limited to the option premium since if the option price is not supported by the market ("in the money"), the buyer will simply allow the option to expire. The seller, however, has an unlimited risk unless she has hedged the risk in some other way. One advantage to an option is that it is lower cost than using futures.

- Over-the-counter (OTC) derivatives — Since the standard provisions of the futures and options markets often do not fit with a specific customer's needs, financial service companies and large marketers offer OTC derivatives that mimic many of the features of the futures/options markets but at different locations and under different terms. A common OTC might be a price ceiling at Topock (the border between California and Arizona) rather than at Henry Hub. In this example, a financial services company guarantees an end user that if she buys gas on the monthly market at Topock, she will never pay more than $4.80. If the price exceeds $4.80, the financial service company will compensate her for the difference between the actual price and the $4.80 ceiling. Another common OTC derivative is known as a price swap. Here someone holding gas (a marketer or producer) subject to market price risk may "swap" the price risk to a financial services company and instead receive a fixed price. OTC derivatives are extremely varied and the products offered can differ widely. Margins and transaction costs, however, tend to be much higher than for futures and options since a financial services company or a marketer is taking on substantial risk of price fluctuations.

Value at Risk

Whatever means is being used to manage risk, it is critical for management of a company to actively measure the aggregate risk level it has incurred on at least a daily, if not an hourly, basis. The risk that is measured is the risk to the company's expected earnings stream if certain movements in market price or other detrimental events were to occur. This aggregate risk is measured by creating a "book" that shows all physical and financial transactions, and estimating the earnings impact of various potential price movements. Procedures must also be in place to catch unauthorized actions of employees who may be trading outside of the guidelines given by management or employees who accidentally make execution mistakes. We are all too familiar with the potential for huge impacts caused by the failures in risk management.

A common way of measuring aggregate risk is called Value at Risk (VAR). In industry jargon, VAR can be described as "the expected loss for an adverse market movement with a specified probability over a particular period of time." In layman's terms, VAR is a calculation that attempts to assess how much total risk a company has taken over any given period.

Unfortunately, VAR is only an imperfect means of quantifying actual risk. To calculate VAR, an assumption is made as to what level of market volatility will be experienced and then a level of statistical certainty is chosen (often 95%). Given a 95% certainty, your actual Value at Risk will theoretically exceed your calculation 18 days out of the year (5% of the time). And if one of these 18 days is a day when gas prices spike due to market forces, you can lose a lot of money quickly! In reality, one number cannot adequately reflect the complex risks encountered in today's marketplace. Thus it is always important to understand that the level of risks in the marketplace are inherently high, and that no means of analysis or use of risk management techniques can fully hedge all risks.

Despite this caveat, VAR is useful for a number of purposes:

- Quickly quantifying risk associated with a specific transaction.

- Comparing risk associated with expected return for alternative transactions.

- Quantifying risk across a portfolio of transactions (rather than looking at each transaction individually).

- Evaluating overall corporate risk profiles.

- Setting limits on allowed risk either by specific trader, specific business unit or corporate-wide.

As the industry becomes more familiar with the risks associated with the gas business, new measures that go beyond VAR are being developed. More detailed methods including Extreme Value Theory, Stress Testing and Back Testing are used to supplement the basic risk estimates available from VAR. But in the end, risk management will always include a significant amount of art in addition to the statistical methodologies!

What you will learn:

- How the upstream, midstream and downstream sectors may evolve

- A vision for a sustainable energy future

12

SECTION TWELVE: THE FUTURE OF THE GAS BUSINESS

As we have seen in this book, the gas industry has faced radical changes in the recent decades. Once structured by long-term arrangements and heavily regulated, much of the business is now a thriving commodity marketplace characterized by daily price fluctuations and competitive trading. And it appears unlikely that we've reached the apex of change. On the horizon are continued commoditization of supply and transportation, competition in all market sectors, convergence of gas and electricity, continued mergers, cost-cutting strategies, the rise of LNG, and concerns over supply availability. In the long run, we are likely to see less dependence on regulatory controls, greater dependence on market forces, the emergence of retail energy merchants, and the development of a global supply chain.

The one thing we can be assured of is that the gas business will continue to see frequent change. While no one can predict a precise course of events, a look at ongoing trends and past experience in other businesses gives us some indication of what we might expect.

A Review of Market Changes

Less than 30 years ago, transportation and supply services were bundled and all commodity and transportation prices were regulated from wellhead to burnertip. Interstate pipelines purchased gas supply from producers and aggregators and re-sold that supply to LDCs. LDCs then re-sold the gas to end users. Today, the gas world is much less controlled and much more complex. Many customers now enjoy a myriad of service options and continue to benefit from decreases in the price of gas. Gas supply, and to some extent transportation, has entered the commoditization phase of the market maturation cycle. Meanwhile, other parts of the business such as local distribution remain fully regulated. Supply prices, which fell significantly in the first 15 years of deregulation, have recently skyrocketed to historic highs. These high prices, coupled with concerns over the availability of future supplies, have led to strong efforts to develop non-traditional North American reserves and the infrastructure to import more supplies via

LNG. And consumers are being forced to carefully evaluate their usage patterns and the potential for investments in energy efficiency.

The Future of the Upstream Sector

As this book goes to press in late 2005, there is great concern in the U.S. as to whether traditional natural gas supplies will continue to keep up with rising natural gas demand. Most studies agree that our traditional sources of supply will satisfy only a portion of future gas needs with remaining needs being met by new supplies from areas such as Alaska, Arctic Canada or overseas by LNG. Uncertainties regarding supply have resulted in increasing gas prices that have remained above historical levels for the last three winters. And despite a large number of drilling rigs active in the basins, we have yet to see a surge in supply to ameliorate high prices.

The debate is on as to whether this means we are running short on new sources of natural gas or whether other factors are temporarily constraining a market response to high prices. Given what we know about the size of the natural gas resource worldwide, it appears that the latter is a more accurate reflection of reality. Huge natural gas supplies exist globally, though the delivery infrastructure does not exist to make these resources widely available to the U.S. The future of gas production may move beyond a focus on a regional market designed to serve just the U.S. and Canada, and may instead become focused on natural gas production to serve a global marketplace. It's not so far fetched that the increasing need for supply production in North America may be replaced by a global trade in LNG – similar to today's oil marketplace. Countries with vast natural gas resources including Russia, Iran, Nigeria, Qatar, Saudi Arabia, and the United Arab Emirates may become tomorrow's global natural gas titans, rivaling today's major oil producers. In such a scenario, global gas production will be dominated by major multi-national corporations who will focus on technological and cross-cultural business expertise with huge balance sheets to finance projects across the globe. Given the cost of developing infrastructure to deliver these reserves to market, it is likely that such well-financed majors will also take on the task of building the necessary international pipelines and strategically placed LNG terminals.

In the longer run we may see development of the robust natural gas hydrates resource. Hydrates are ice crystals that trap methane molecules, and form below a depth of about 400 feet below the ocean. Some scientists believe that huge amounts of natural gas exist locked in methane hydrates. But production will depend on expensive technology advancements and most researchers believe exploitation of such resources is at least 25 years in the future.

The Future of the Midstream Sector

The gas pipeline business has become perhaps the most stable of the gas sectors in today's marketplace. Generally consistent regulation and rising demand has resulted in consistent earnings. Yet at the same time, the gas trading and financial services sectors are experiencing a period of restructuring. New market leaders are expected to emerge in the next few years, perhaps led by cash-rich merchant banks or renewed activity by the international energy majors.

As we look further into the future, we can envision an increasingly competitive business driven by global forces and increasing competition in the retail sector. Under this scenario, gas marketing will likely become dominated by the international energy majors who will control global natural gas supplies and exercise market power far beyond any one national government's control. As the market evolves, the pipeline sector is likely to once again be shaken out of today's more stable environment and forced to reinvent the gas transmission business. Perhaps the future will lead to integrated national energy transmission networks that remove the need to focus on transmission nominations and paths. Such networks may take delivery of gas molecules and/or electrons at one location and offer a service in which energy is delivered at another location – in any form desired by the consumer. The challenge of moving gas and/or converting it to electricity will be left to the energy network.

The Future of the Downstream Sector

Somewhat like the pipeline sector, LDCs have recently stabilized under the umbrella of relatively predictable regulation. Utility commissions that a few years ago were pushing for market restructuring and introduction of retail competition are suddenly skeptical of the benefits of deregulation given the turmoil in the electricity industry. But like the gas pipelines, LDCs may be experiencing the lull before the next storm. Deregulation initiatives are moving quickly in other places in the world, especially in the European Union where all gas and electric customers are scheduled to have supplier choice by the end of the decade. Global retail marketers with experience in Europe are quietly becoming active in U.S. and Canadian markets as are marketing arms of the major oil companies. As the electricity marketplace stabilizes, we may see renewed activity by well-financed electricity companies that will attempt to displace gas sales with new electro-technology. Given regulatory and institutional constraints, LDCs will have difficulty responding. Thus, in the next five years we may see a renewed push for deregulation and customer choice at the retail level.

A Sustainable Energy Future?

Many believe that our hydrocarbon-based society will one day be replaced by a society based on hydrogen fuel. In fact, the vision of a hydrogen future has been embraced not only by academics and environmentalists, but also by the European Union, many major oil companies and U.S. policymakers. Hydrogen is a fuel that stores energy effectively, burns highly efficiently and leaves minimal emissions after combustion. Of course, significant barriers to a hydrogen future exist, including technology development and conversion of our current energy infrastructure. And we have to figure out how to extract hydrogen without using technologies that create the same issues we have with today's energy sources. Yet advancements may be closer than many believe. The country of Iceland has announced it will become the world's first oil-free country, replacing all fossil fuels with clean-burning hydrogen. This concept is now receiving

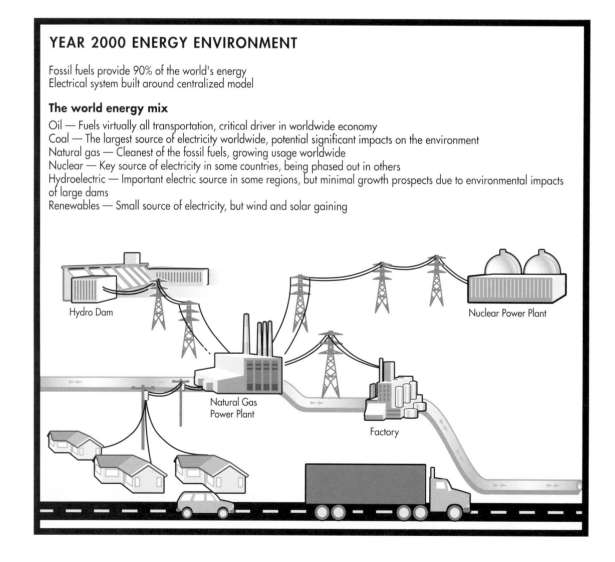

YEAR 2000 ENERGY ENVIRONMENT

Fossil fuels provide 90% of the world's energy
Electrical system built around centralized model

The world energy mix

Oil — Fuels virtually all transportation, critical driver in worldwide economy
Coal — The largest source of electricity worldwide, potential significant impacts on the environment
Natural gas — Cleanest of the fossil fuels, growing usage worldwide
Nuclear — Key source of electricity in some countries, being phased out in others
Hydroelectric — Important electric source in some regions, but minimal growth prospects due to environmental impacts of large dams
Renewables — Small source of electricity, but wind and solar gaining

Hydro Dam

Nuclear Power Plant

Natural Gas
Power Plant

Factory

financial support from the European Union as well as corporate giants such as DaimlerChrysler and Royal Dutch/Shell.

One potential scenario (illustrated below) would replace today's centralized electric generation system with a more distributed system based on fuel cells and solar energy located at end-use locations. Automobiles would also be powered by fuel cells and might even act as home generators when parked in the garage. Wind and photovoltaic resources would contribute clean power and natural gas-fired generation may become a source used only for peaks. Hydrogen might be created from water using energy sources such as wind power or new generation nuclear. Hydrogen might also be created from natural gas at the wellhead and the current natural gas pipeline infrastructure

YEAR 2050 ENERGY ENVIRONMENT

Fossil fuels no longer dominate
Renewables are important source of world's energy
Electrical system converted to distributed model with significant use of cogeneration
Hydrogen used as energy storage and transport medium
Efficiency of end-use devices has significantly increased

The world energy mix

Wind — Extensive network of wind farms becomes key source of electricity
Solar — Distributed network of solar cells provides electricity at users' locations
Natural gas — Still used for peaking electricity needs, remainder of resource devoted to hydrogen production
Nuclear — New breed of reactors may become important source of baseload electricity
Hydroelectric — Important electric source for peaking and system support, but environmental concerns and lack of undeveloped resources limit growth
Hydrogen — Hydrogen extracted from water or natural gas has replaced oil to fuel transport and has replaced natural gas as fuel for space and water heating.

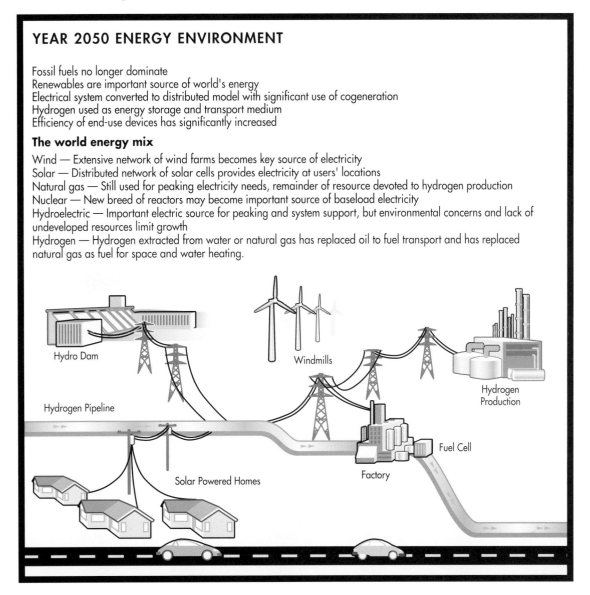

Hydro Dam

Windmills

Hydrogen Production

Hydrogen Pipeline

Fuel Cell

Factory

Solar Powered Homes

could be upgraded to transport hydrogen. Hydrogen would then be piped to end users as a replacement for natural gas and fuel oil, and as a fuel for the ubiquitous fuel cells.

In the meantime, we must find a way to bridge the gap between today's world and the long-term future. The attractiveness of natural gas as a clean-burning fossil fuel makes it an ideal bridge fuel to transition us to a sustainable long-term future. Yet increasing demand for natural gas in the U.S., Europe and Asia has led to supply tightness and high prices in the consuming countries. Ample reserves exist worldwide, and the key to accessing them will be the development of global infrastructure and markets as well as stable regulation that will allow these reserves to be used effectively. Also important will be ongoing efforts to promote energy efficiency so that resources are used wisely.

Natural gas, whose mythic beginnings prompted creation of the Oracle of Delphi, enters the 21st century as a potential bridge fuel to environmentally benign hydrogen and a renewable energy based economy. As the industry evolves, there is no doubt that its progress will continue to be marked with vast change and exciting technological and business developments. The future will be driven by the creativity and knowledge of individuals who expend the time and energy to become experts not only in the natural gas industry, but also in the broader areas of sustainable development and serving customer needs through continual innovation.

12

A

APPENDIX A: GLOSSARY

Abandoned well — A gas well that is not in use because it was originally a dry hole or because it has ceased to provide gas in economical quantities.

Allocation — The priority system used by a pipeline to distribute transportation capacity among customers when available capacity is less than nominated volumes.

Aggregator — An entity that collects smaller packages of gas from producers and markets them in larger packages.

Aquifer — A geologic formation containing water. Natural gas is often found in the presence of aquifers.

As-available service — See Interruptible service.

Associated gas — Natural gas found in contact with or dissolved in crude oil.

Alternative fuel vehicle — A vehicle that can operate on a fuel other than gasoline or diesel fuel.

At-risk construction — A pipeline expansion or new construction that accepts (on behalf of its owner) the risk of cost underrecovery.

Backhaul — A transaction in which gas is delivered upstream of the point at which it was received into the system. Since gas cannot physically move both ways in a pipe, backhaul service is a paper transaction rather than actual physical movement of gas.

Balancing — The act of matching volumes of gas received by a pipeline or LDC to the volumes of gas removed from the pipeline or LDC at the delivery point.

Balancing account — A regulatory convention in which costs and/or revenues associated with certain LDC or pipeline expenses are tracked.

Base load — Natural gas usage that is constant throughout a specified time period.

Basis differential — The difference in price between an index and the cash price of the same commodity. Often basis is used to refer to the difference in price between an index based at a trading hub and the cash price at another physical location.

Bid week — The period near the end of each month when the bulk of contracts for monthly gas supply for the following month are finalized.

British thermal unit (Btu) — The quantity of heat required to raise the temperature of one pound of water by one degree Fahrenheit.

Broker — A third party that earns a profit by matching a gas buyer and a gas seller. Unlike marketers, brokers do not take ownership of the gas.

Bundled service — Gas sales service and transportation service packaged together in a single transaction in which the LDC, on behalf of its customers, buys gas from producers or marketers and delivers it to them.

Burnertip — The point where gas is consumed.

Butane — A component of natural gas that is typically extracted at a processing plant and sold separately.

Bypass — The purchase and transport of natural gas by an end user through a direct connection to an interstate pipeline, rather than the local distribution company (thereby avoiding LDC charges).

A

Capacity — The maximum amount of natural gas that can be produced, transported, stored, distributed, or utilized in a given period of time.

Capacity brokering — The assignment of rights to receive firm transportation service.

Capacity release — The right (authorized by FERC Order 636) of a firm transportation holder to assign that capacity on a temporary or permanent basis to the highest bidder.

Cap rock — An impermeable rock layer that prevents gas from escaping out of a trap.

Carbon dioxide — A by-product of natural gas combustion and also an impurity sometimes found in natural gas.

Citygate — The point at which gas is received into the LDC distribution system.

Coalbed methane — Any gas produced from a coal seam.

Coal gas — See Manufactured gas.

Cogeneration — Production of two forms of energy at once, commonly electricity plus steam or hot water.

Collections — The act of getting customers to pay their bills.

Commodity — Anything that is bought and sold in a highly competitive market.

Commodities typically have many buyers and sellers, are very liquid and subject to fluctuation in price according to supply and demand. In the natural gas business, commodity is sometimes used as a synonym for the natural gas molecules going through a meter.

Compressed natural gas — Natural gas that is compressed for use in vehicles and other applications (but not related to a pipeline).

Compressor — Machinery used to increase the pressure of natural gas on a pipeline system.

Compressor station — A facility that propels gas through transmission lines or into storage by increasing pressure.

Condensate — Hydrocarbons that are gaseous under reservoir conditions, but become liquid at the wellhead.

Confirmation — The notification received by a customer from a pipeline indicating how much of a specific nomination has been scheduled.

Core customers — Residential and small commercial customers who generally lack alternatives to gas service.

Cost of service — The total amount of money, including return on invested capital, operation and maintenance costs, administrative costs, taxes, and depreciation expense required to provide a utility service.

Creditworthiness — An evaluation of a customer's or trading partner's financial accountability.

Curtailment — Cutting gas service to customers when supply is not sufficient to meet demand.

Cubic foot — A common gas volume measurement. The amount of gas required to fill a volume of one cubic foot under stated conditions of temperature, pressure and water vapor.

Cushion gas — A volume of gas that must always be present in a storage field to maintain adequate pressure to cycle gas.

Customer charge — A fixed amount paid by a gas customer regardless of demand or energy consumption.

Cycling — Injecting and withdrawing gas from storage.

Deliverability — The amount of natural gas a well, field, pipeline, or distribution system can supply in a given period of time.

Delivery point — The location on a pipeline to which gas is transported.

Demand — The rate at which gas is delivered to or by a system at a specific instant or averaged over a period of time.

Demand charge — Also known as a reservation charge, the portion of a transportation or storage rate that reserves space on the facility, and is based on contract quantity (paid regardless of whether or not service is taken). For end-use rates, the demand charge may refer to a charge based either on contract quantity or the maximum demand experienced in a given billing period.

Deregulation — The process of decreasing or eliminating government regulatory control over industries and allowing competitive forces to drive the market.

Distribution system — A gas pipeline normally operating at pressures of 60 pounds per square inch or less that brings gas from the higher pressure transmission line to the customer.

Downstream — Commercial gas operations that are closer to the market.

Dry gas — Natural gas that doesn't contain liquid hydrocarbons.

A

Electronic bulletin board (EBB) — An electronic service that provides information about a pipeline's rates, available capacity, etc. and on which third parties can bid for capacity.

Emergency Flow Order (EFO) — An order by a pipeline to users of natural gas to restrict usage in order to maintain the integrity of the system. Generally follows an Operational Flow Order.

Enhanced oil recovery (EOR) fields — Reservoirs in which secondary recovery techniques are used to extract oil.

End user — The ultimate consumer of gas.

Energy Services Company (ESCO) — A company that provides services to end users relating to their energy usage. Common services include energy efficiency and demand side management.

Ethane — A component of natural gas.

Exploration — The process of finding natural gas.

Feedstock — Raw material such as natural gas used to manufacture chemicals made from petroleum.

FERC — The Federal Energy Regulatory Commission, the federal body that regulates interstate transmission of gas and electricity.

Firm service — The highest priority sales, supply, transportation, or storage service that is the last to be interrupted in times of shortage.

Fossil fuel — Any fuel created by the decomposition of organic matter, including natural gas, oil and coal.

Fuel Cell — A device that converts stored chemical energy directly to electrical energy. Although similar to a battery, the major difference is that a fuel cell operates with a continuous supply of fuel (such as natural gas or hydrogen) as opposed to a battery which contains a fixed supply of fuel.

Futures contract — A supply contract between a buyer and seller where the buyer is obligated to take delivery and the seller is obligated to provide delivery of a fixed amount of commodity at a predetermined price and location. Futures are bought and sold through an exchange such as NYMEX.

Gas Industry Standards Board (GISB) — An industry group comprised of pipelines and created by the FERC whose mission was to standardize operating and scheduling procedures nationwide. Now part of NAESB.

Gas marketer — The middleman between gas supply and end user who typically takes title to the gas and resells it to end users with a variety of other services.

Gathering system — A system of small pipelines that collects gas from individual lease facilities for delivery to a mainline system.

Heating value — The amount of energy content contained within a specific volume of natural gas. Commonly measured in units of Btu per Mcf.

Hedge — The initiation of a transaction in a physical or financial market to reduce risk.

Henry Hub — A pipeline interconnect in Louisiana where a number of interstate and intrastate pipelines meet. The standard delivery point for the NYMEX natural gas futures contract.

Homogenous products — Products that the customer sees as basically the same.

Horizontal drilling — New technology in which the well bore is horizontal when it penetrates the reservoir.

Hub — A physical location where multiple pipelines interconnect and where buyers and sellers can make transactions.

Hydrocarbon — Chemical compound containing carbon and hydrogen.

Imbalance — The discrepancy between the amount a customer contracts to transport or consume and the actual volumes transported or consumed.

Impermeable rock — Rock that does not allow gas or fluid to migrate through it.

Incentive ratemaking — See Performance-based ratemaking.

Index — A calculated number designed to represent the average price of gas bought and sold at a specific location.

Injection — The process by which natural gas is forced back into a reservoir for storage purposes.

Interconnection — The facilities that connect two pipelines.

Interruptible service — Also called as-available service, this storage or pipeline service is only available after all firm customers have been served and system conditions permit additional volumes to be moved.

Interstate pipeline — A federally regulated pipeline that is engaged in moving gas in interstate commerce.

Intrastate pipeline — A pipeline that is regulated by the state public utilities commission. Intrastate pipelines cannot transport gas that will ultimately be delivered outside the state in which the pipeline is regulated.

Lease facility — The facility in a production area where gas from a specific lease is collected, where condensate and water are separated from the gas, and where gas is metered as a basis for compensating lease participants and royalty holders.

Line pack — The inventory of natural gas in a pipeline.

Liquefied natural gas (LNG) — Natural gas that has been chilled to the point that it liquifies. LNG is used as a means to store and transport natural gas.

Load factor — The ratio of the amount of gas used over a period of time in comparison to the maximum amount the customer can use.

Local distribution company (LDC) — The regulated distribution company that moves natural gas from the interstate pipeline to end-use customers and often provides bundled gas supply service to residential and small commercial customers.

Looping — Increasing capacity on a pipeline system by adding another pipeline that is parallel to existing lines.

Mainline system — A gas pipeline normally operating at pressures greater than 60 pounds per square inch, that transports gas from other mainline systems or gathering systems to lower pressure distribution and local transmission systems. Also known as a transmission line or backbone system.

Manufactured gas — A combustible fuel produced by burning coal. Manufactured gas was used primarily in lighting.

Market center — A physical location where buyers and sellers make transactions (this may or may not also be a hub).

Market segmentation — A two-step process of identifying broad product markets and dividing them up to select target markets and develop suitable marketing mixes.

Marketer — An entity that buys gas, arranges for its transportation and then resells the gas to end users or other gas purchasers.

Marketing — The performance of activities that seeks to accomplish the organization's objectives by anticipating customer needs and profitably satisfying those needs through delivering products and services.

Marketing affiliate — Typically a non-regulated marketing company with corporate ties to a regulated pipeline or LDC. Regulated companies are prohibited from favoring marketing affiliates in any business transactions.

Market power — The ability of a market entity to artificially elevate prices over a period of time.

Mercaptan — A harmless odor injected into natural gas giving it the smell of rotten eggs.

Meter — A device used to measure natural gas as it moves from one point on the system to another.

Methane — The main component of natural gas.

Midstream — Commercial gas operations that are generally associated with the transmission aspect of the industry.

Mileage-based rates — Rates based on the actual distance natural gas is transported.

Monopoly — A marketplace characterized by only one seller with a unique product.

Muni — See municipal utility.

Municipal utility — A utility owned and operated by a municipality or a group of municipalities.

Natural gas — A combustible gaseous mixture of simple hydrocarbon compounds, primarily methane.

Netback — A calculation determining the amount of money a seller will realize in the producing area once all transportation charges have been subtracted from the market price.

Netforward — A calculation determining the total cost of gas in the market once the commodity price in the producing area plus all transportation charges have been added.

Nomination — A request to transport a specific quantity of gas on a specific day under a specific contract.

Noncore customers — Relatively large customers who have alternate fuel capability such as large commercial, industrial, cogeneration, and electric generation customers.

No-notice service — A transportation service that allows customers to receive gas on demand and without an advance nomination.

Non-performance — Failure to deliver according to the terms of a contract.

North American Energy Standards Board (NAESB) — An industry group of energy companies created to standardize operating and scheduling procedures for natural gas and electricity across North America.

Notice of Proposed Rulemaking — A document released by a regulatory agency in which the agency sets forth a proposed revision to its rules and gives market participants notice concerning the regulatory proceeding that will consider these revised rules.

NYMEX — New York Mercantile Exchange, the organization that provides the market for trading of natural gas futures and options.

Odorization — The process of adding an artificial odor to natural gas so that leaks can be detected.

Off-peak — The period of a day, week, month, or year when demand is at its lowest.

Open access — The requirement that pipelines transport or store gas for any creditworthy party on a non-discriminatory basis.

Operational Flow Order (OFO) — An order by a pipeline to users of natural gas to restrict usage in order to maintain the integrity of the system.

Option — A contract that gives the holder the right, but not the obligation, to purchase or sell a commodity at a specific price within a specified time period in return for a premium payment.

Order 636 — An order issued by FERC in 1992 laying out the final blueprint for interstate gas industry deregulation, including the unbundling of gas sales and transport services, implementation of capacity release, recovery of transition costs, and changes in transportation rate design.

Peak — The period of a day, week, month, or year when demand is at its highest.

Peak load — The maximum demand for gas in a given period of time (usually monthly or annually).

Performance-based ratemaking (PBR) — Ratemaking in which a base rate is set and rate changes occur only due to a specified mechanism. The utility takes the risk of costs higher than allowed by the mechanism but also has the potential to benefit if costs are lower than assumed. Also called incentive ratemaking.

Permeable rock — Rock that has spaces through which gas or fluid can migrate.

Permeability — The ease with which a fluid or gas can pass through rock.

Pig — A device used to clean and inspect the inside of a pipeline.

Producer — An entity that operates wells to bring gas from reservoirs into the gathering system.

Production — The process of extracting gas and processing it so that it is of usable quality.

Propane — A component of natural gas that is typically extracted at a processing plant and sold separately.

Pro-rata allocation — Methodology that allows all customers to receive the same proportion of gas available as their share of total firm contracted volumes.

Proved reserves — The quantity of natural gas that is economically recoverable with the use of current technology.

Public Services Commission (PSC) — The state agency that regulates local distribution companies and intrastate pipelines.

Public Utilities Commission (PUC) — See Public Services Commission.

Public utility — A regulated entity that supplies the general public with an essential service such as electricity, natural gas, water, or telephone.

Rate base — The net investment in facilities, equipment and other property a utility has constructed or purchased to provide utility service to its customers.

Rate case — The regulatory proceeding where a pipeline or LDC's rates are determined.

Rate design — The development and structure of rates for gas supply and service for various customer classes.

Rate schedule — Commission-approved document setting out rates and terms of service specific to a certain service and service provider.

Receipt point — The point on a pipeline system at which gas is taken into the system.

Regulation — The myriad of rules or orders issued by state or federal agencies that dictate how gas service is provided to customers. Note that this term is also used in gas operations to describe the act of managing gas pressures in the pipe.

Reservation charge — See Demand charge.

Reserves — The quantity of natural gas existing in underground formations.

Reservoir — An underground deposit of natural gas.

Resources — Quantities of gas – discovered or undiscovered – that can reasonably be expected to exist.

Retail marketer — A firm that sells products and services directly to end users.

Return on investment (ROI) — Ratio of net profit after taxes to the investment used to make the net profit.

Revenue requirement — The revenues a pipeline or LDC must take in to cover its total estimated costs and allowed return.

Rules — Commission-approved general terms of service included in tariffs.

Scheduling — The process of confirming nominations and, if necessary, using priority rules to determine which gas can flow under system constraints.

Service territory — The geographical area served by a utility.

Shipper — Any party that contracts with a pipeline for the transportation of natural gas and retains title while it is transported.

Shut-in well — A well that has been completed but is not currently producing gas.

Speculating — The initiation of a transaction in a physical or financial market with the goal of making a profit due to market movement.

Spot market — The short-term market for natural gas.

Storage — A means of maintaining gas in reserve for future demand, either through injection into a storage field or by holding it within the pipeline (known as line packing).

Supply basin — A geographical area where numerous reservoirs are located.

Take-or-pay — A contractual provision that requires a shipper to pay for service whether it was utilized or not.

Tariff — All effective rate schedules for a pipeline or LDC, along with the general terms and conditions of service.

Therm — A unit of heating value. One therm is equivalent to 100,000 Btu.

Three-dimensional (3-D) seismic technology — Similar to a CAT scan, technology that uses sound waves to paint a three-dimensional picture of the earth's geologic formations.

Throughput — The volume of gas flowing through a pipeline.

Trading point — See Market center.

Transmission — The process of transporting large volumes of natural gas over long distances.

Trap — An area of the earth's crust that has developed in such a way that it traps petroleum.

Unbundling — The separation of a pipeline company's or LDC's transportation services from gas procurement services.

Upstream — Commercial gas operations that are generally associated with the production aspect of the industry.

Usage charge — A component of a pipeline's or LDC's rate structure charged on a per unit of usage basis.

Value at Risk (VAR) — The expected loss for an adverse market movement with a specified probability over a particular period of time.

Well — The hole drilled into the earth's surface to produce natural gas.

Wellhead — The point where gas is pumped from the reservoir and enters the gathering system.

Wet gas — Natural gas that produces a liquid condensate when it is brought to the surface.

Working gas — Natural gas in a storage field.

Zone rates — Rates based on the distance gas is transported.

APPENDIX B: UNITS AND CONVERSIONS

Mcf = Thousand Cubic Feet

MMcf = Million Cubic Feet

Btu = British Thermal Unit

MMBtu = Million Btu

GJ = gigajoule (metric measure of energy)

Dth = decatherm

1 therm = 100,000 Btu

1 Dth = 10 therms

10 therms =1 MMBtu

1,000,000 Btu = 1 MMBtu

1 Dth = 1 MMBtu

1000 Mcf = 1 MMcf

1000 MMcf = 1 Bcf

1 MMcf = 1,015 MMBtu*

1 GJ = . 95 MMBtu

*This conversion varies with the energy content of the gas.

C

APPENDIX C: ACRONYMS

AGA — American Gas Association

ALJ — Administrative Law Judge

Bcf — Billion cubic feet

Btu — British thermal unit

Cf — Cubic foot

CGA — Canadian Gas Association

CNG — Compressed natural gas

CPCN — Certificate of Public Convenience and Necessity

DOE — U.S. Department of Energy

Dth — Decatherm

EBB — Electronic bulletin board

EIA — Energy Information Administration

EDI — Electronic data interchange

EFO — Emergency Flow Order

EOR — Enhanced oil recovery

EPA — Environmental Protection Agency

EPCA — Environmental Policy Conservation Act of 1965

ESCO — Energy services company

FERC — Federal Energy Regulatory Commission

FPA — Federal Power Act

FPC — Federal Power Commission

GISB — Gas Industry Standards Board

GJ — Gigajoule

GRI — Gas Research Institute

HVAC — Heating, venting and air conditioning

INGAA — Interstate Natural Gas Association of America

IOU — Investor-owned utility

IPAA — Independent Petroleum Association of America

IPP — Independent power producer

IT — Interruptible transportation

LDC — Local distribution company

LNG — Liquefied natural gas

LPG — Liquefied petroleum gas

MAOP — Maximum allowable operating pressure

Mcf — Thousand cubic feet

MDQ — Maximum daily quantity

MFV — Modified fixed-variable

MMBtu — Million British thermal units

MMcf — Million cubic feet

MMDth — Million decatherms

NARUC — National Association of Regulatory Utility Commissioners

NEA — National Energy Act of 1978

NEB — National Energy Board (of Canada)

NGL — Natural gas liquids

NGA —Natural Gas Act of 1938

NGPA — Natural Gas Policy Act of 1978

NGSA — Natural Gas Supply Association

NGV — Natural gas vehicle

NOPR — Notice of Proposed Rulemaking

NYMEX — New York Mercantile Exchange

O&M — Operations and maintenance

OBA — Operational balancing agreement

OFO — Operational Flow Order

PSC — Public Services Commission

Psi — Pounds per square inch

Psig — Pounds per square inch gauge

PUC — Public Utilities Commission

PUD — Public utility district

PURPA — Public Utilities Regulatory Policies Act of 1978

R&D — Research and development

ROE — Return on equity

ROR — Rate of return

SCADA — Supervisory Control and Data Acquisition

SEC — Securities and Exchange Commission

SFV — Straight fixed-variable

Tcf — Trillion cubic feet

Th — Therm

USGS — United States Geological Survey

VAR — Value at Risk

WACOG — Weighted average cost of gas

D

APPENDIX D: INDEX

D

D